Mondays, Thursdays

All the material in this book is from my column in the *Daily Mirror* which has been running on Mondays and Thursdays since 1970.

My readers – or such of them as write to me – have asked for it, and now they have got it.

My space in the *Mirror* was formerly occupied by the great Cassandra. I have always been conscious of his shade glowering over my shoulder and would never dare touch on any of his pet themes. The reader anxious to hear about cats, eggs, puns, cookery (including soups) and the old Euston Station had better look up the vintage files.

But if he wants to know about trams, tin toys, childhood games, blackberrying, Christmas traumas, my grandmother, the new Euston Station and how cities ought to be built, it is all here.

K. W.

KEITH WATERHOUSE

Mondays, Thursdays

London
MICHAEL JOSEPH

First published in Great Britain by Michael Joseph Ltd
52 Bedford Square, London WC1
1976

ISBN 0 7181 1480 9

Set and printed in Great Britain by
Tonbridge Printers Ltd, Peach Hall Works, Tonbridge, Kent
in Plantin eleven on twelve point on paper supplied by
P. F. Bingham Ltd, and bound by James Burn
at Esher, Surrey

Contents

Mondays, Thursdays

Underneath The Lamp Light

I had a nasty shock the other day. I went back to the street where I was brought up and found that the lamp-post was missing.

There was a lamp-post there all right a concrete clothes-prop fizzing pale-blue mercury and bathing the neighbourhood in shadowless light – very efficient, and for those within its pale orbit undoubtedly the next best thing to having a council house in the Sea of Tranquillity.

But the lamp-post I remember, *the* lamp-post – a squat, cast-iron pillar painted bright green, surmounted by a hissing gas-lantern that flickered behind four square window panes like a stranded lighthouse – was gone for ever. This is my requiem for it.

You must understand that it was more than a source of light. Our lamp-post was, to begin with, a highly functional object. Protruding from its iron neck was a stout metal bar, the official purpose of which was to support the ladder of the man who came to mend or clean the gas-mantle.

This metal bar was perfect for tying bits of rope to, swinging from, doing somersaults over, throwing pieces of slate at, or merely dangling from by two puny arms while your friends counted slowly to a hundred and you felt that you were on the rack.

Because of its basic usefulness to us the lamp-post was the pivot of our community. It was our maypole, roundabout, assault course, market place, moot and general headquarters.

It was the wicket for our cricket matches, one side of a goal mouth, the base for rounders and a complicated game called 'Relieve-oh!' which rarely got further than a shrill quarrel about its devious local rules.

We played marbles under our lamp-post, tested our conkers against its hollow, clanking base and shinned up it to light Woodbines and sparklers, or merely to experience the heady smell of singed hair.

The fraternity of our lamp-post, like an officers' mess or a gentleman's club, had a rigid system of protocol. No one was admitted to membership under the age of three; no one from other streets was allowed except as a guest; cry-babies, boy scouts and anyone wearing glasses were rigorously blackballed.

Ladies' night was on Fridays, when the girls of the street, hungry for adventure, hung about under that shining orb like tiny Lili Marlenes.

Our lamp-post was the venue for all the main social events of the year.

In high summer we sat beneath it poking tar bubbles in the road with long sticks or trying to prise up the lid of the storm-drain that was supposed to give you scarlet fever.

In November we assembled around it to count our fireworks and decide whether the Big Banger or the Jumping Cracker should be poked through Old Mother Teaker's letter box.

At Christmas we used it as a boundary post to divide the carol-singing concession between those whose voices had broken and those who could still bring a fine treble to the first two lines of 'Away in a manger'. But the social attraction of the year in our street was the Button Fair, and this was invariably staged beneath our lamp-post. This always followed the annual bank holiday fair that was held on an acre of waste-ground nearby; having lost all our pennies on the roll-'em-down stalls we would hurry home and chalk up our own stalls on the pavement, using buttons for money.

8

Different kinds of buttons had different values: a trouser button was the lowest denomination, a jacket button was worth two trouser buttons, an overcoat button was worth three, and a cloth-covered button snipped surreptitiously off your sister's best coat was worth four or even six for a big one.

Sometimes urchins from other streets tried to gatecrash the Button Fair with handfuls of shirt-buttons snitched from their mothers' work-boxes, but these were rejected as being worthless foreign currency.

If you had comics to swop at any time of the year, you stood under the lamp-post with your rolled-up merchandise tucked into your stocking; eventually a fellow-trader would come out with his stock of *Radio Funs* or *Knock-Outs* and haggle with you – one *Knock-Out* for two American Dick Tracey comics (they were a drug on the market at that time), or one *Radio Fun*, mint condition, for an incomplete copy of *Illustrated Chips* and a cigarette card of Don Bradman.

The best time around our lamp-post was on autumn evenings, after the rain. You looked gloomily out of the window, tired of Meccano and Dinky toys and craving human company. You'd see the gas-jet flicker and go on magically, by itself; its bouncing reflection would light up the puddles and tell you that the rain had stopped.

Out of the shadows would stroll some boy from up the street, looking about him, eager for companionship.

You'd watch him loafing around under the lamp-post and pray that he wouldn't go indoors again before you'd struggled into your raincoat. You'd hurry out and hang about with him, abstractedly discussing sex or football or floating a matchbox down the gutter, but all the time keeping a sharp look-out on the doors for signs of life.

Soon other figures would emerge from the shadows, and soon after that the whole street would be alive with boys: diving through the wet privet hedges, swinging like Tarzan from the iron bar of the lamp-post, whooping and whistling and yodelling, running in and out of that friendly pool of light.

As I said, our lamp-post has disappeared now. The concrete column that replaced it is far more serviceable and it probably holds a silver medal from the Road Safety Council. But there were no children playing beneath it when I passed. Where were they, I wonder? Watching television, or doing homework, or

9

joining in constructive games in an adventure playground?

Has the magic gone out of childhood – or is it just that my generation were lucky possessors of a magic lamp?

Down Memory Lane By Tram

As one who believes nearly all city planners to be more or less certifiably mad, I was surprised to see that a group of them had turned up an intelligent solution to urban traffic problems.

The idea is a very simple one: a light, fast-moving, single-car railway that would operate on the central strip between the dual carriageways, connecting far-flung suburban districts with city centres.

I like to imagine the inventors of this ingenious system snapping their fingers and trying to think of a name for their revolutionary vehicles.

'Eureka!' shouts one of them, leaping out of his bath one morning. 'Let's call them trams!'

Trams. Is there anyone who has ever travelled on those rocking, roaring, rattling monsters and doesn't sometimes long to see them back again?

Can you remember that peculiar, pungent smell of burning tin, that soothing whine like the sound of a Messerschmitt making a forced landing; the mournful, clanking bell as the workmen's special loomed up through the fog?

Have you ever been to the Transport Museum at Clapham Common and shed a tear for that splendid, marooned flotilla of electric land-galleons, still able and ready, by the look of them, to rumble out into Clapham High Street and sink every new-fangled London bus in sight?

Their brass still gleams, their livery of red and blue and chocolate brown is spotless; port and starboard, fore and aft they bristle with armour in the shape of tin-plated advertisements for Bovril and Mazawattee Tea.

I was brought up on trams. My earliest memory is of being taken by older children to the top of the street to watch them go hissing by, of picking hot pebbles up from the tramtracks and sucking them, of putting halfpennies on the lines to see them flattened.

I was sick on my first tram at the age of four, and was impressed by the foresight of the Leeds City Transport Engineer (whose signature appeared in gold letters on every tram, like a personal guarantee) in providing sand, bucket, brush and shovel for my especial benefit.

I ran away from home by tram at the age of ten, and covered an incredible distance for a penny – a winter cruise it was, out past the allotments and the greyhound stadium, through the city centre, then out of home waters into the tropical delights of the municipal golf-course, strange heathen parks and infidel suburbs I'd never seen before.

The terminus – where trams shuttled backwards and forwards on a single track and new drivers came on duty with impressive tin boxes containing their lunch and ship's papers – had all the bustle and excitement of New York harbour.

I would readily have believed in those days you could traverse the globe by tram.

You could certainly get as far as Bradford by taking a tram to the city boundary, walking through a sort of frontier post equivalent to the Brandenburg gate, and putting yourself at the mercy of the unfamiliar, plum-liveried Bradford tram that was touting for passengers a hundred yards away. It was one of the perils of the big outside world.

But there was always something faintly perilous about a voyage by tram, even when it flew the reassuring colours of Leeds City Transport Department.

It rolled and swayed alarmingly on one-in-four gradients, and negotiated hairpin bends with the abandon of an Irish tea-clipper racing the Cutty Sark.

And sometimes the trolley-pole would become disconnected from the overhead wires and the tram would lie puffing and steaming like a stranded whale, while the harassed conductor prodded and tormented it with his 15-foot-long harpoon.

For all that, it was a cheap and usually efficient system. There was no rubbish about timetables – if you missed one there was always another.

Occasionally, indeed, if somewhere along the route an unhappy cyclist had held up traffic while struggling to free his front tyre from the tramlines, there might be a convoy of six or even twelve.

Riding by tram was an unflagging source of interest. There

was, apart from anything else, an incredible variety of different types of tram, and it was always a matter of keen speculation which particular model would come steaming up next.

There were open-topped trams with fretted galleries and so many ornamental loops and scrolls that they looked like mobile follies built for an eccentric Edwardian millionaire.

There were streamlined modern trams with gigantic, impressive cow-catchers that looked as if they could scoop up a Ford Popular and toss it on the nearest scrap-heap.

There was a heavy-duty tram for football crowds, that seemed to be constructed of pig-iron.

There was even an illuminated tram which cruised aimlessly about Leeds during the summer months, festooned with thousands of electric light bulbs and bedecked with the flags of all nations. I never quite knew the purpose of this – perhaps it was just municipal high spirits.

It vanished at the beginning of the war, when all the blue trams were painted in camouflage khaki and looked more like battleships than ever. Daily we expected Lord Haw-Haw to announce that the German fleet had sunk the Ark Royal and the No. 10 tram to Elland Road.

You could have fun on a tram, if you were young and irresponsible. If it was an open tram you could perch on the outer deck in the freezing cold and hang over the side to the consternation of passers-by.

You could wind the handle of the destination board so that it read: 'Depot only'.

You could run down the length of the tram knocking back the reversible back-rests of the slatted seats with a satisfactory clacking noise.

And instead of walking sedately down the spiral stairs you could slide down a brass pole like a bear on a stick.

But the greatest joy was in looking at trams. Just observing them. Standing on a busy shopping street in the evening drizzle, listening for the melancholy bell, then watching that great tin dinosaur, bathed in a creamy light, come lumbering into sight, hissing and steaming, squelching over pea-pods outside the greengrocer's.

When trams began to disappear there was, in most cities, a touching farewell to them. Their trolley-poles were hung with bunting, the Lord Mayor turned out in his chain of office, and people fought for the privilege of riding the last mile on the last tram.

Somehow, I can't see that happening when they knock off the buses.

Those Radio Times

I have been listening to the wireless again. Not the radio. Not that transistorised plastic matchbox which sings and burps and prattles all day long like a drunken mynah bird, but a real wireless set.

It's a mahogany cabinet the size of a small wardrobe, its loudspeaker is framed by a fretwork fleur-de-lis, and it has strange stations on the dial like Daventry, Hilversum, Zagreb, and Paris (Eiffel Tower).

A friend of mine bought it for two pounds ten in the Portobello Road, and together we tried to get it going. An important accessory had been mislaid somewhere – the complete set comes with a 70-foot pole and half a mile of aerial wire – and so the results were not good.

But we did get some excellent oscillation. In fact I haven't heard oscillation like that since I was ten years old, just back from the corner garage with the accumulator topped up and all ready for my weekly appointment with *The Man in Black*.

And we did, for a few seconds, hear a voice. It might have been Jimmy Savile, or it might have been the news in German from Koenigswusterhausen on 1,250 metres.

I prefer to believe that it was Professor C. E. M. Joad uttering his immortal phrase 'It all depends what you mean ...' which has been trapped in the ether for a quarter of a century, to be released like a genie only when someone tunes in that magic mahogany box.

I must confess that I've never quite believed that the golden age of wireless was gone for ever.

I know there's been some kind of reorganisation over at Broadcasting House, and that the Forces Programme has disappeared. But does that mean that *ITMA* is never coming back? Is it true that Jack (*Blue Pencil*) Warner is a television policeman now?

13

When's the next season of *Workers' Playtime*? And what's happened to the dulcet choir who used to sing *It's Monday Night at Eight O'Clock, Oh can't you hear the chimes*?

I'm sure they're all still there, just resting, somewhere between Bournemouth and Daventry, pressed like flowers behind that misty glass dial. Stainless Stephen is there, and Mrs Feather, and Gillie Potter calling England from Hogsnorton, and Grandma Buggins, and Elsie and Doris Waters, and Mr Middleton. Robb Wilton has been there since the day war broke out; Henry Hall is there, and tonight *is* his guest night . . .

And what about that hearty couple with the piano? Not Rawicz and Landauer – the other ones, who used to wake us up at 7 am with physical jerks? Surely they're only waiting for Tony Blackburn to stop telling his rotten jokes before they strike up another tinkling refrain of *Up in the Morning Early*.

Remembering how we all used to sit with our ears glued to the wireless from morning till night, I marvel that any of us have the nerve to castigate our children for their obsession with the telly. The wireless was ten times more addictive.

Its catch-phrases – 'Can I do yer now, sir?' and 'Very tasty, very sweet' and 'Mind my bike' – were on every lip.

You couldn't go through a door without someone piping up, 'After *you*, Claude,' and it was impossible to sit in a music-hall for more than ten minutes without hearing an imitation of Commander ('When I was in Patagonia') Campbell.

When Tommy Handley died it was an occasion for national mourning, and I believe there was some talk of burying him in Westminster Abbey.

I was brought up in the war, and on the pretext that you never knew when they might announce an invasion, the wireless was literally never switched off from *Kitchen Front* in the morning to the national anthems of all the allies at midnight.

Certain programmes were accorded the importance and ceremonial of immovable religious feasts. Everything stopped for *ITMA, Danger Men at Work* and *Hi Gang*. J. B. Priestley's *Postscript* was compulsory listening, and the whole family gathered round for 'Here is the news and this is Bruce Belfrage reading it.'

Then there was *Scrapbook, Have a Go, PC 49, Happidrome* and Sandy Macpherson whenever he chose to be on the air, which if I remember correctly was about twenty-five times a day.

For the rest of the time I was allowed to twiddle the knob and pick up Lord Haw-Haw, or Glenn Miller on AFN, or Radio Luxembourg in the forlorn belief that the Ovaltinies might not be casualties of the war.

I never weaned myself off *Children's Hour*. Given the choice between *Magic Roundabout* and *Toytown*, my loyalty would still belong to Larry the Lamb, Ernest the Policeman and Dennis the Dachshund.

It's curious that the wireless should have had such an impact on us all, when you consider what a snobby medium it really was.

Didn't we ever think it hilarious that they used to dress their announcers in dinner jackets to read the football results? Was there really a national hullabaloo because Wilfred Pickles was allowed to read the news with a faint Northern accent?

Weren't we ever irritated by the urbane, upper-class voices of *Any Questions* and *Woman's Hour*, or by the Cheltenham Ladies' College accents of the children's serials, or by the grovelling cockney whine of all those comic taxi-drivers, kitchen maids and faithful batmen who played the bit parts in *Saturday Night Theatre?*

Didn't we really object to the monumental impertinence of the Reith Sunday, when a sober perambulation through the potted ferns of *Palm Court* was all we were allowed in the way of entertainment?

I suppose, when you think about it, that the wireless as we knew it had to go. It belongs, very firmly, in the dead era of dressing-up for dinner, country-house week-ends, and jumble sales in aid of the poor of the parish.

The peasants were given their treats, of course – we had our *Variety Bandbox* and *Ignorance is Bliss* and *Ack-ack, Beer-beer*. But somehow there was always the faintest whiff of patronage: the suggestion of the squire reluctantly presiding at the village concert.

You always felt that the BBC would have been happier with the Western Brothers affectionately parodying the upper classes, or A. J. Alan telling one of his pointless stories, or Ronald Frankau being suavely offensive about the morals of shopgirls.

But did it *all* have to go? Isn't there *any* programme worth enshrining in mahogany, to be picked up faintly on five-valve sets in Bratislava, Breslau and Klagenfurt?

What was wrong with *In Town Tonight?* What have they
done to Revnell and West, not to mention Oliver Wakefield?
Why, when I switch on my radio, do I always get Dave Cash
instead of the night-watchman sitting round his fire-bucket outside the Old Town Hall?

Will Lord Hill (who does not for one minute persuade me
that he is anyone other than the Radio Doctor) kindly look into
this? And if he can bring back oscillation while he's about it,
so much the better.

No Flowers By Request

I invite you to join me in mourning the death of my begonia;
suddenly, at its lodgings on my window-sill. The cause of death
was multiple contusions. The verdict is manslaughter.

Begonia Rex was its full name, but the title was hereditary
and an embarrassment to its self-effacing owner. Of a retiring
disposition, my begonia never sought to assert itself by flowering,
and was indeed so diffident that it was often mistaken for a
clump of rhubarb.

I hope it has gone to a better and sunnier world than this.
It had lived under my roof longer than any other green thing,
the previous record being held by a spider plant which expired
of aspirin poisoning at the tender age of 28 days.

Begonia Rex was roughly a year and seven months old but I
do not know exactly when or where it was born, for to tell the
truth it was adopted. It may be that it was an illegitimate
begonia, found abandoned in the left-luggage office at Victoria
Station. I bought it for two pounds five from the local nursery-
man.

No questions were asked. No adoption society checked up
on me. I was handed my begonia in its swaddling clothes of
grey papier mâché, and I bore it home.

It took ill immediately.

Its knobbled leaves dropped and shrivelled in upon themselves
like nervous armadillos.

Its stems bent over at an angle of 180 degrees as if trying
to make urgent contact with Mother Earth.

I watered it, placed it in the sun and fed it liquid manure

in discreet quantities. My begonia languished. I gave it up for lost and put it out by the dustbins for the final rites.

Two days later I went down to the yard and a miracle had happened. My begonia, lying face downwards in less than 16 ounces of earth, was struggling to life.

Well, perhaps not so much struggling as pawing feebly in the general direction of the sun. One leaf was definitely cocked upwards in an attitude of hope. A stalk reached out in a cork-screw motion as if seeking an exit from the charnel-house.

My begonia was reborn.

I nursed it better. I polished its leaves with milk. I took it into the garden for short walks. I watered it every hour on the hour.

It began to die on me again. Deliberately and languorously, in broad daylight. Its milk-nurtured leaves curled hopelessly and fell, and every one was a fluttering reproach.

I called in a friend who is an expert on the good earth and the things that grow in it.

'You are drowning the bloody thing,' he said.

I said I didn't know plants could drown. He said that plants could die of practically any malady known to man. He specified malnutrition, heart disease, lack of vitamin C and gross personal neglect. He added that my begonia looked as if it had suffered from all these complaints in its short existence, but what it currently needed was a life-jacket.

I took the hint and went easy on the water. My invalid begonia was soon off the danger list.

It thrived and grew fat. Then, without warning, it stopped thriving and grew thin again. It wilted, this time at an alarming rate. It seemed hell-bent on self-destruction.

Convinced that I had a suicidal begonia on my hands, I consulted the oracle.

'Strangulation.'

'But I haven't laid a finger on it.'

'The bloody plant-pot,' he said, 'is too small. Your begonia is growing up. It hasn't room to breathe.'

I bought a bigger plant-pot and performed a successful trans-plant operation. I felt like a horticultural Christiaan Barnard as I watched Begonia Rex pass the crisis.

That was the last time it gave me trouble. It was ill again, frequently, but it was a grown-up begonia now and able to look after itself. We were still good friends but we saw less of each other.

The other day my begonia was out on the window-sill and I forgot it was there. I forgot that the window cleaner was coming.

One swipe with a chamois leather and my begonia lay mortally wounded in the concrete area four floors below. I hurried down but I was too late. Begonia Rex was beyond recall.

We'd come a long way together. The place seemed empty without it and I remembered that when people lose a dog they're advised to get another quickly. So I went back to the nurseries.

Begonia Rex is dead.

Long live Begonia Rex.

Who's Taking Our Mickey?

Have you ever spent a rainy afternoon in central London looking for Mickey Mouse with a seven-year-old boy?

Don't. Teach him snakes and ladders instead.

There was a time when Mickey Mouse was easy to locate anywhere in England and, if you couldn't find him, there was always Pluto. If Pluto was on leave of absence there was Bugs Bunny or Tom and Jerry.

Not any more.

You begin your damp search at the Eros Cinema in Piccadilly Circus which used to be one of half a dozen cartoon theatres in the West End. It is a cartoon theatre still, but, because of the weather, it is full.

At this point you should go home. However, you remember another cartoon theatre across the road. You lead your son through the blinding rain and you are confronted by several glossy stills of ladies without their clothes on.

The last time you were in this cinema it was to see Popeye the Sailor Man. Today they are showing an X film called 'Heterosexual'.

There's a news theatre in Coventry Street that used to put on Tweety Pie festivals. Your son places a wet paw in yours and you squelch off in that direction. The programme is 'Man of Violence' and 'Naked England'.

There is another news theatre in Charing Cross Road where they specialised in the old cowboy serials and the odd Three Stooges.

Today they specialise in 'Love Variations' and 'Mister Kinky'. The seven-year-old asks if Mister Kinky is the funny man who's short-sighted and you say No, that's Mister Magoo.

The thunder rolls and you splash on towards a cinema in Trafalgar Square where you used to watch Goofy and Woody Woodpecker. They are showing 'She Lost Her You Know What'. The lightning flashes and illuminates an enormous placard of a naked woman.

At one time you could have sat all day in that place and not even seen a naked rabbit.

The other cartoon cinema you remember is showing 'The Queer' and 'The Sadist'. But you have promised an afternoon treat and so you end up drying-out in a Wimpy bar opposite a pornographic bookshop.

You wonder if Mickey Mouse is still making a living.

Down With Uvnarbrasp

If you couldn't get to Mexico for the World Cup or Edinburgh for the Commonwealth Games, perhaps you can make the next sporting marathon, which is in London next month.

The finals of the National Crossword Puzzle championship.

With pencils sharpened, anagrams polished and the name of a large Australian bird of three letters scribbled on their cuffs, a thousand competitors will fight down and across a puzzle of Olympic specifications.

I shall not be among them.

In order to qualify you had to solve a series of eliminating puzzles in *The Times*. To my everlasting shame, I cannot do *The Times* crossword.

I will tell you something else. I cannot do the *Mirror* crossword either. I have been wrestling with the damn thing for twenty years and I have never completed it once.

The *Mirror* puzzle, as you know, comes in two flavours. There is the quizword for those who have at their fingertips the name of the great snake killed by Apollo at Delphi. There is the plain crossword for those who thought Apollo was the name of a West End theatre.

That's the one for me. The one that keeps it simple.

I always start well with a brisk sprint through the 'Across' department. One across, a confused fight in seven letters. Easy. The word is quarrel. A table game, also in seven letters? Snooker, obviously. A Cornish city in five letters? It's got to be Truro.

As long as I'm working at horizontal level I can get through the puzzle at lightning speed. It's when I switch to the vertical position that I run into trouble. For some reason, they always make the 'Down' clues more difficult.

Two down. Smuggled goods. Ten letters.

All right, let's look at the letters we've already got filled in. $U*N*R**A*P$.

What the hell kind of a word is that?

UBNERGRASP? ULNORPEALP? UPNERTRAMP?

There must be *some* word that fits. Think it out, now. Smuggled goods in ten letters.

After considerable thought I put down *UVNARBRASP*, which for all I know is Russian for contraband.

Devilish crafty, these crossword compilers.

My Tin Heaven

The tin car was in the window of Mrs Bailey's toyshop for exactly four weeks.

It was a silver racing car with a number four on the side and a tin driver in the bucket seat and a tin key that wound it up. The price asked was one and elevenpence-halfpenny, which was Mrs Bailey's way of saying two bob.

Tin car number four was the bestest toy I had ever seen. I wanted it. I got it. Four weeks was how long it took me to save up that one and elevenpence-halfpenny.

The linoleum on the scullery floor became the track at Brooklands. The clothes-peg basket by the mangle stood in for the crowded grandstand. A baking-tin under the gas stove was pressed into service as the pits.

I played with tin car number four for hours and days and

weeks and months. Circuit by circuit and lap by lap, I learned that it was a highly lethal toy.

If you sucked it, which I did, you were in danger of lead poisoning from the paint. If you tinkered with it, which I did, there was a strong chance that the clockwork spring would unwind and put your eye out. If you shoved your finger into the bucket seat, which I did, it came out bleeding.

Tin car number four scratched like a cat and nipped like a lobster but it was my favourite.

The spring bust and the key bent and an offside wheel came off and the driver lost his tin head in a pile-up with a flat iron. After skidding around the lino for a full year my tin car finished up in – but where did those tin toys finish up? They just vanished, presumably into a clockwork heaven.

Last Saturday I passed an antique shop which specialises in the toys of yesteryear. Among the Victorian dolls and Edwardian rocking-horses was the exact replica of tin car number four. It was, in fact, tin car number seven.

The paint was scratched and a wheel had gone askew but the driver's tin head was still intact and the car was beautiful and I wanted it.

The price asked was nine pounds.

Lock your children's playthings away. Confiscate the Lego, bank the Meccano and put the Matchbox cars in the safe deposit.

Those aren't toys, they're investments.

Golden Days Of Rubbish

For some people it's the smell of apples on the bough or newly-baked bread. For me it has always been the smell of freshly-mixed cement, wet mortar and boiling tar.

I'm talking about those delicate, elusive, siren odours that waft you back into childhood. I walked past a building site on a hot afternoon last week and at once I was transported thirty-five years back in time.

Some of the happiest days of my life were spent pouring buckets of water into a pile of builder's sand and pretending I was at the seaside.

I've never regretted that mine was a city childhood. We never knew the delights of swimming in a river or riding in hay-carts. But there were newts to be caught in the corporation reservoir, and dams to be built across the festering stream that carried effluent from the dye-works.

We stole nails by the hundredweight from the clerk of works' yard. We became bronze-tanned in the equatorial heat of the watchman's brazier where we melted down strips of purloined lead. The scent of hot tar, putty and cement, all mingled, was as heady as May blossom.

There were expeditions to the slag heaps where, equipped with a dustbin lid, you could slide down a Cresta Run of smouldering ash.

There was a limestone quarry from which we emerged after a morning's reconnaissance looking like the Homepride flour graders.

There were the indoor swimming baths, smelling pungently of carbolic and Bovril.

And there were always golf balls to be 'found' on the municipal links. Scooping a golf ball out of a bunker and disappearing at the speed of light into the sanctuary of the rhododendron bushes was one excitement. The other was cutting into your loot with a sharp penknife and seeing what came out.

If you were unlucky, it was a putrescent, sticky, white fluid that was said to be liable to burn your hand off if you touched it. If you were fortunate, it was a tightly-bound ball of elastic with easily a thousand uses if only you could think of them.

There were raids to be carried out on the local rubbish dump which, at that time of year, had the languorous, heavy atmosphere of a tropical swamp.

Bluebottles hovered lazily over the clumps of deadly nightshade that flourished in a compost of rotting cardboard; city-orientated bees carried rust-like pollen from one abandoned bicycle frame to another.

We risked typhoid and cholera, but there were valuable trophies in that steaming urban jungle. One week we bore home a bus tyre, taking it in turns to roll along the main road curled up inside it.

Another time we found an enormous cache of used typewriter ribbons, and for weeks they fluttered from the telegraph wires like streamers after the biggest Mardi Gras in history.

We preferred marbles in the dustbowl of the school play-ground to climbing trees in the bluebell woods, and the asphalt perimeter of the park bandstand to the treacherous grass beyond it.

Which is not to say that we were ignorant of the lore of the countryside. We knew that all red berries are poisonous, that ladybirds bring you luck and picking dandelions makes you wet the bed. But at the end of the day we were urban creatures by instinct and inclination.

At harvest time we liked to forage for used tram tickets around the terminus. If it had been a good summer they lay clean and thick on the ground, all sky-blue or deep green, or white with a broad red band signifying a workman's return – as rare and precious as a thrush's egg.

The sun blazed, the unidentified birds sang, and all the anonymous flowers bloomed.

For us, the true, deep joy of summer was playing whip-and-top on the melting tarmac, drinking Tizer straight from the bottle, and the welcome bell of the Walls' ice cream man. And the limestone quarry, the golf links, the rubbish dump and the corporation reservoir.

Huckleberry Finn, you may believe me, didn't have it any more golden.

The Good Picnic Guide

The subject is picnics. Please take notes, and smoke if you wish. We will kick off by defining not what a picnic is, but what a picnic is not.

A picnic is not a feast of cold chicken, tomato salad, pickles, tongue, ham and warmish white wine consumed off a damask tablecloth in a field, wood or spinney.

Such a meal is only a portable business lunch, eaten at a table without legs and thus – unless you happen to be Japanese – liable to give you indigestion. Anyway, you've forgotten the mayonnaise.

A picnic is not sandwiches. Nor is it vacuum-flasks and greaseproof-paper bags in a car parked on a cliff top with the windows up.

Nor is it hampers, spirit kettles, portable barbecues, collapsible stools, storm-proof field-ovens or any other kind of Ideal Home Exhibition alfresco gadgetry.

What, then, is a picnic?

The following elements are indispensable:

ONE: Children. A picnic without children is like roast beef without Yorkshire pudding. Children are the whole delight and purpose of a picnic, as well as coming in useful for fetching cigarettes.

TWO: Glorious weather. This is vital, for picnics and mackintoshes do not go hand in hand. Picnics were intended to be eaten under a blue sky, with wasps in attendance.

THREE: A good site. There is a lot more in this than finding a meadow with fine, springy grass and its fair ration of butter-cups. There must be streams to fall in, trees to fall out of, hills to roll down, and preferably a mad bull somewhere in the offing This gives picnicking its proper air of adventure.

FOUR: The right food. The following recipe is culled from a lifetime's experience and will yield a successful picnic for four people.

You get four small, deep carrier bags of the kind that are used by wine merchants to hold one bottle of Scotch.

Into each carrier bag you place these ingredients:

One banana. One orange. One small portion of processed cheese. One handful of assorted biscuits, plain and sweet. One packet of chewing gum. One sausage roll. One bag of potato crisps. One hard-boiled egg. Some cheese straws. A screw-top bottle of fizzy lemonade. One gingerbread man. One bun. One bar of chocolate. One stick of barley sugar.

And other items to taste, provided that they are not boringly wholesome, that they were not left over from yesterday's dinner, and especially that they are not placed between two slices of bread, whether brown or white.

You hand out the carrier bags to your squad of picnickers and you set off.

You do not worry if the oldest one, who has been crazed with hunger ever since finishing breakfast ten minutes ago, commences to eat his picnic before the car is even out of the garage.

You do not worry if the youngest one eats his chocolate before he gets to his sausage roll, or even if he eats his sausage roll at all.

You do not worry about your children getting sticky.

You do not worry about your children feeling sick.

You do not, in fact, worry about anything. You park the car and step out briskly into the countryside. You find a suitable spot. You sit down. You act as arbitrator while your children set up a brisk barter trade in boiled eggs and bananas.

You eat. Your children begin to eat, cease eating in order to catch dragonflies and resume eating after they have fallen in a bog.

You do not warn them against germs or about indigestion.

You light a cigarette.

The sun shines on.

You fall asleep. All is rustic and peaceful except for the occasional magic cries of small picnickers being stung by wasps.

When it is time to leave, you heave your discarded carrier bags into the nearest litter bin and return home unencumbered by rugs, vacuum-flasks or wicker shopping baskets containing milk bottles and unwanted bread.

You will feel bloated and dyspeptic for your picnic will have been stodgy, messy and almost totally lacking in vitamins. But it will have contained the one ingredient that no successful picnic can afford to be without.

It will have been memorable, I promise you.

It Was All On The Cards

Did you happen to know, by any happy chance, that the baby orang-outan rides upside-down on its mother's back as she swings through the jungle?

Or that Rochester Castle is one of the finest examples of Norman military architecture in England? Or that the sheldrake is essentially a coast-bird, usually making its nest in a rabbit burrow among sandhills?

My unimpeachable references for these and other supremely useless facts – such as one that W. Coggins was once a notable goalkeeper for Bristol City – are 'Zoo Babies', 'Views of Interest', 'Curious Beaks' and 'Famous Footballers'.

They're all the titles of cigarette cards which were issued between 1930 and the outbreak of World War II. I dug them out when I read that thousands of cards are to be sold by auction at Caxton Hall this week.

Yes – auctioned! And we used to pick them up at tram-stops.

What the going price of ciggy cards is in this age of gift coupons and green stamps I've no idea, but they can hardly be more valuable than they were to me when I used to collect them.

I don't know how I could have survived my early years without cigarette cards. They were my education, my sustenance, my currency and my source of fortune.

With a single card from a Player's set of fifty English cricketers you could keep the school bully at bay or get your homework done. With three rare examples of Godfrey Phillips's 'Russo-Japanese War' (a series of twenty) you could buy friendship.

With a complete set of John Sinclair's 'Champion Dogs' you had a swap for a second-hand cricket bat. Or a roller skate. Or the earth itself, and the moon and the stars (series of forty-eight) and the Koh-i-noor Diamond ('Famous Jewels' – series of fifty).

Ogden, Carreras, Gallaher's, Cope's, W.D. and H.O. Wills – their names, to us, were like vintage labels to a wine snob. 'Wild Flowers' were rarer than 'Radio Celebrities', and one 'Champions of Sport' was worth two 'Famous British Trees'. No connoisseur, spitting out rare port in a sawdust cellar, could have matched our expertise.

I never owned a full set myself, and I don't think I ever met anyone who did. Wild rumours occasionally went round that some smarty-boots or other had the complete run of 'Fifty British Locomotives', all neatly mounted in a penny album.

When it came to an independent audit though, it always turned out that he had two Flying Scots and no Brighton Belle.

But it was all good fun, provided that two gummed cards didn't get stuck together – a recurring tragedy.

What the tobacco companies hoped to get out of our enjoyment I can't imagine. We swapped their cards, we scoured the gutter for their cards, we accosted complete strangers and begged their cards. But we never bought their cigarettes.

Did Wills' Woodbines really increase their sales with 'Gems of Italian Architecture'? Did Churchman's win over the smoking public with 'Landmarks in Railway Progress'? Did the tobacco kiosks ring with cries of 'Cancel my Craven "A" and give me ten Player's – they've just started a series of "Curious Beaks"?'

Nowadays, of course, you save up your coupons and they send you a set of teak-handled steak knives. It's probably a better commercial proposition – but where's the coupon that will tell us more than we could possibly want to know about the Old English Sheep Dog? ('Our Puppies', Number Thirteen).

And how, now that cigarette cards have gone, will future generations ever learn that the crown of Charlemagne weighs fourteen pounds? ('Famous Crowns', Number Nine).

The Trying Dutchman

A lady whose job in life is to feed computers (what on, I wonder? Human sacrifices?) takes issue with me over some remarks I made on the infinite capacity of these monsters for dropping electronic bricks.

Computers, this punch-card kennelmaid tells me flatly, do not make mistakes. It is the frail mortals who operate them who make mistakes.

She reminds me of a motto which is apparently quoted wherever computers meet: 'Garbage in, garbage out'.

I accept this reproof, which incidentally goes a long way to explain my unsatisfactory relationship with Flash Hans, the illiterate computer from Amsterdam.

Flash Hans is the push-button equivalent of a Warren Street used-car salesman. He came into my life two years ago with an offer of Dutch bulbs. When I did not rise to the bait of tulips by post, Flash Hans switched tactics and began touting a consignment of unreadable books in what he called good-to-touch binding.

Over the months he has also tried to make a quick killing in the fields of records, magazine subscriptions, cut-price posters and a greenhouse which you can assemble in the comfort of your own home.

During this protracted one-way correspondence, Flash Hans has addressed me consistently as *K. WATREHOLNE 12496*, which is not my name. I finally wrote to him pointing this out, at the same time asking whether 12496 was the computerised version of the OBE.

Flash Hans did not respond immediately but some weeks later he sent me, in quadruplicate, a never-to-be-repeated offer of the recorded works of Beethoven. All four of these incredible bargains were addressed to *K. WALTERHOSE 12496.*

Anyway, thanks to my correspondent, the mystery is now cleared up. Behind the computer which can't spell is a button-pushing Dutchman who can't spell either.

I note with humility what the keeper of Flash Hans's English cousin tells me – that by 1990 nearly all business will be done by computers and I will just have to learn to live with them.

I only wish she hadn't addressed her letter to KIETH Waterhouse.

A Toothsome Tuck-in

There was fizzy pop and there was jelly and there were plum duffs as round as footballs and there were mounds of pies and there were fruit bowls overflowing with grapes, but most of all there was sausage and mash.

Bangers and mash, you could say, were greatly in evidence. The potatoes were heaped in great fluffy mountains and the bangers protruded at all angles like crags on Snowdonia.

A single, succulent, sizzling sausage was pronged on the fork of the honoured guest, who could have been anyone from a vagrant in rags to a tiger in a suit of pyjamas.

The venue was the Hotel de Posh. The occasion was the routing of swag-carrying burglars by Weary Willy and Tired Tim or by Alfie the Air Tramp or by the Bruin Boys. The reward was a slap-up feed (or munchful meal) and a bag of cash (or oof) labelled £££'s .

There was, in the happy realm of the old-style comic papers, a perfect sense of order and justice such as you rarely encountered in the bleak streets outside the Editor's Den.

That, I suppose, was why they occupied so much of our time. 'Everything is safe, solid and unquestionable,' wrote George Orwell. 'Everything will be the same for ever and ever.' He was writing about the Magnet and the Gem, but could have included Comic Cuts, Illustrated Chips, the Joker, the Jester, Film Fun and a dozen more.

I'd always felt guilty about the womb-like attraction of those pink and blue and green pages until I read the other day that Mr Peter Dickinson, the author of several highly-respected children's books, has heartily recommended comics as an important part of the child's reading diet.

Comics, says the excellent Mr Dickinson, help a child to unwind from the demands of more serious reading.

For a child, says the incomparable Mr Dickinson, real intellectual freedom is reading a pile of old comics under the bed on a sunny afternoon.

I always knew it was, but I wanted it in writing. So they were not wasted after all, those enchanted, kneecap-mottling hours by the fireside, when I pored over my Yuletide Bumper Numbers or Eggciting Easter Specials. And there never was any real danger that I'd end up illiterate from reading Inky the Office Boy's Chortling Nu Yeer Messidge.

Thank you, Mr Dickinson, and bless you. Pray accept this fat cigar, this fistful of fivers, this diamond winkle-pin and this free invite to a mirthful movie. Perhaps we can sally forth later for a toothsome tuck-in at the Hotel de Posh.

When The Chips Are Down

Dialogue in a restaurant:
Waiter: And would you require some vegetables, sair?
Me: Yes, please. Chips.
Waiter: Certainly, sair. *Pommes frites.*
Me: No. Chips.
Waiter: I understand, sair. French fried potatoes.
Me: No. Chips.

This waiter, a Spaniard, had within eighteen months of landing upon these blighted islands been completely and utterly brainwashed by the suburban middle classes.

Chips, along with toilet, telly, condiments, comfy, lounge, serviette, have you had sufficient, beg pardon and pleased to meet you is one of the top ten non-U expressions of all time. Which is very curious when you consider that there is not an eating house in Britain, from the ritziest Ritz to the tattiest roadside caff, that does not serve potatoes in this nourishing form, and there is no home, stately or otherwise, without its chip pan.

Chips are our national dish, as endemic to the English as sauerkraut is to the Germans.

And yet the humble murphy, when peeled, sliced, and deep fried at a temperature of 360 degrees Fahrenheit, divides this nation as nothing has done since the flight of Charles I from the Roundheads.

Observe the dedication with which the residents of an estate of bungalows will combine, petition and campaign to prevent some honest trader opening a fish and chip saloon in their vicinity. Arnold Wesker wrote a play in which a priggish, middle-class character fulminates against some East End work people because they insisted on ordering chips with everything. To be sure, Wesker's object was to illuminate the poverty of ambition of the working class. But can you imagine an Italian sounding off against his fellow-countrymen for ordering spaghetti?

It goes without saying that this is the most snobbish country on the face of the earth. If you go into the average hotel cocktail bar the one thing they won't serve you is beer, although it is our national drink. If you ask for a cup of tea after your dinner in even a moderately expensive restaurant you'll get some very curious looks. Menus are printed in a language that not one person in ten can comprehend.

The only logical purpose of all this mumbo-jumbo is to bewilder, frighten and confuse those who are not used to it – in other words to keep the chip-eaters out in the street. For the difference between chips and *pommes frites* is more than a delicately semantic one. It is the difference between cloth caps and bowlers, between the public bar and the tennis club.

One of the most disgusting aspects of living in this country is that anything identified with the 'working class' is supposed to be funny, common or vulgar. Horse-racing is okay but dog-racing is supposed to be coarse. Braces are funny because they hold up workmen's trousers. Coach outings are common because working-class people go on them. Chips are funny, common *and* vulgar because working-class people eat them with their fingers along the Golden Mile at Blackpool.

We're supposed to have had a social revolution since the war but I sometimes think that you could have fooled me. The assumption all along has been that working-class institutions, working-class customs, working-class preferences have no value at all.

The working man has opportunity, it's true, but it's the opportunity to stop being what he is. His children can go to grammar school and lose their accents. He can take his family abroad for their holiday but we'd rather he drank the wine of the region instead of light ale, even though the wine of the region makes him vomit. He can save up his money and buy a semi-detached, but we expect that he'll resign from the working man's club and start wearing a collar and tie when he takes the dog for a walk.

In the United States, as the immigrants got richer, they took their tastes with them – which is why you can have tomato sauce with your hamburger in the most expensive restaurant in New York. In England, you're supposed to leave your origins behind you.

I'm inclined to suspect that, consciously or not, the 'social revolution' in this country was never a working-class movement at all. Its object, it seems to me in glum moments, was to strengthen, widen and consolidate the middle-classes – probably the most stultifyingly boring, bigoted, pigeon-brained collection of people ever assembled together since primeval man uttered the first grunt.

Why else would a respectable Lancashire mill-worker be proud of his son for no other reason than that he wears a white collar? Why would people whose homes belong to a building society erect a wall across the street to separate themselves from those whose homes belong to the city council? Why else is the English dream not of owning the factory but of getting the hell out of it and running a pub or a tobacconist's shop?

In spite of everything they say about productivity and all the rest of it, work, when you get right down to it, is still a four-letter word – and there is an actual apartheid in operation against those who do it as compared with those who plan it, urge it or profit from it. This is still the land of workmen's entrances and executive lifts, of 'staff' restaurants and works canteens, of clocking-in for blue-collars and signing-in for white collars.

The expression I've been using, 'working-class', is, of course, a very old-fashioned one, except among those who really do the work. It reminds the rest of us of night-schools, insurance clubs and the *Morning Star*. Politicians, Labour and Tory, won't use the term – they, too, they *especially*, have their sights fixed on a middle-class, scampi-eating, technological meritocracy.

But it seems to me that this country has a long way to go before equality is available in equal portions. When you can really order chips with everything, I'll believe that the social revolution has arrived.

Bred Any Good Books ?

I have books the way some people have mice. My shelves bulge with them. The floorboards groan under their weight. They have invaded the best armchair and the dining-table and are now engaged in a pincer movement on the wardrobe.

I am over-run by reading matter. Correction. I am over-run by printed pages cut into quarto, octavo, duodecimo or tricesimo-secundo and bound in leather, marbled boards, crushed morocco or limp cloth.

But no one could call the bulk of this material readable.

When, and why, did I acquire the Army and Navy Stores catalogue for 1929? How did a pre-war directory of wire trades come into my possession? What am I doing with six bound volumes of the *Radio Times*?

My theory is that they breed. There is a book on Japanese armour in my literary knacker's yard which I swear was not there a week ago. It was either born on my shelves or it is an illegal immigrant.

Another explanation may be that I am incapable of ever walking past a second-hand bookshop. Having entered, I pick up the nearest volume. Having picked it up, I am incapable of letting go of it. Sooner or later, I tell myself, this survey of granite quarries is bound to come in useful.

Yesterday I came across a book-barrow that was having its winter clear-out. And there, in one corner, were half a dozen fat, tempting books under a sign reading: 'Free – take them away'.

Treasure galore. Volume one of a Russian novel, in Russian; an out-of-date guide to Leicestershire; a history of the Peninsular

War with the cover missing; a primer on Gregg shorthand; a book of poems by a Victorian clergyman; and a treatise on sugar-boiling. Just what I needed.

But you know what it's like when you're told to help yourself – you feel a bit self-conscious. So I sauntered round the stall a bit, whistling tunelessly to myself and waiting for the other browsers to look the other way.

I had just swallowed hard and was about to grab the loot and run when this down-at-heel character sidled in front of me. A flash of bony wrists and my golden treasury of the world's most useless literature was gone – obviously in the direction of the nearest waste-paper depot.

I felt like a bibliophile who has seen his copy of the Gutenberg Bible eaten by goats.

I didn't want to go away empty-handed so I plonked down two bob and picked out a nice thick tome as a consolation prize.

There was something vaguely familiar about it and when I got home I checked my creaking shelves. I was right – I'd got it already.

I may have missed out on the treatise on sugar-boiling but I bet I am the only man in London with two copies of 'Who's Who' for 1934.

Any takers?

The Figure In The Woodpile

I wonder if Mr Enoch Powell is as concerned as I am about the way this country is being flooded with statistics. All the signs are that statistics are increasing faster than anyone believed possible.

From a mere trickle of births, marriages and deaths at the turn of the century, uncontrolled statistics have multiplied at such an alarming rate that we have now reached a point where everything that can be set down in figures, from the annual yield of fat pigs in Lincolnshire to the production and consumption of slab zinc in Northern Ireland, is wilfully and recklessly tabulated.

I have heard dreadful stories of whole towns being overrun by statistics, of people having to move house because of the number of graphs, tables and monthly averages in their once-respectable neighbourhoods.

Indeed, one lady told me that she had actually had statistics pushed through her letter-box.

In front of me is the Annual Abstract of Statistics just published by the Stationery Office. It contains two and a half per cent more statistics than the 1969 edition, thus showing that the Government has been criminally optimistic in its assessment of what the growth-rate would be.

Entire areas that were once statistic-free – the estimated traffic on all roads in Great Britain, for example, or numbers of employed persons analysed by industrial groups, or the United Kingdom short and medium-term borrowing returns – are now contaminated by the arithmetical cancer in our midst.

On present trends, unless something is done now to send these figures back where they came from – with Government grants if necessary – there will be something like seventy thousand billion statistics roaming free in our lifetime.

Despite all the evidence of the debilitating effect of statistics on our national life – the noxious smells emitted from the cooking of the balance of payment figures, for example – there are those who claim that statistics are not in themselves harmful.

No woman, say these apologists, has ever been raped by a productivity chart.

I advise my critics to look across the Atlantic for, in numerical terms, our statistics will be of American proportions long before the end of this century.

I see a river running with population returns broken down by age, sex, creed and colour. I see a future when there will be statistics on every corner, in every school and pub, even under old ladies' beds.

If that doesn't scare you, of course, I'll just have to think up something else.

The Folly And The Ivy

Panicking? Who's panicking? Anyone'd think I'd never done any Christmas shopping before.

I tell you, I've got it organised.

Look, all I've got to do is choose presents for eighteen people, right? And there's still seven shopping days to go, right?

No, I haven't forgotten the turkey. I shall be getting the turkey on Monday. AND the mince pies. AND the pudding. AND the nuts. AND the Christmas cake.

What do you mean, when do I think I'm going to get any work done? They're only groceries, for God's sake. All right, so I'll have to go to five different shops – they're still only groceries.

I shall set off at 9 a.m. with two carrier bags and work my way down the High Street in a calm and orderly manner. The Christmas groceries will be on these premises all present and correct, by 9.15.

Yes, damn it, including the pork pie.

And the chocolate log.

And the jellies.

And the mandarin oranges.

Not to mention the marzipan fruits that nobody eats anyway, the bacon-flavoured crisps, the sage-and-onion stuffing, the single cream, the double cream, the brussels sprouts, the chestnut purée, the Turkish Delight, the after-dinner mints, the sausages, the five different kinds of cheese, the salty biscuits, the glacé cherries and the Alka-Seltzer.

How do you *think* I'm going to carry the holly? How do I always carry the holly?

No, I'm not forgetting something.

Of course I'm not forgetting the booze. Do I look like a man who forgets the booze?

I shall get the booze on Tuesday.

Thank you, I'm quite aware that the office party is on Tuesday.

The office party does *not* go on till three in the morning. The office party will be over, at the very outside, by four in the afternoon.

From the off-licence, of course – where else would you expect me to get the booze from? The butcher's?

I shall keep a taxi waiting, that's how.

There will be absolutely no question of cruising round the West End at three in the morning looking for an off-licence. I shall buy the booze at four in the afternoon from my usual wineshop. The taxi-driver will help me bring it up the stairs.

The taxi-driver will *not* have to help me up the stairs. I can assure you of that.

Christmas presents? What Christmas presents? Oh, *those* Christmas presents.

I shall do that on Wednesday morning.

Rubbish. A child of three could choose Christmas presents for eighteen people. It's a simple question of not dithering, that's all.

Well they'll just have to have what they're bloody given, won't they?

I *know* the shops will be crowded. I *expect* the shops to be crowded. I shall just barge into Selfridge's, pick up the first eighteen wrapped gifts I come across, and barge out again.

Ah, now I'm glad you mentioned the Christmas tree, because that's all taken care of.

On Wednesday, that's when. On the way back from Selfridge's.

Yes, for crying out loud, with eighteen parcels! Well they'll have to be *small* parcels, won't they?

I *can't* make two journeys for the simple reason that on Wednesday afternoon I have to go to the Sunday School nativity play. In any case, don't forget I promised to attend that Christmas lunch.

I have never turned up drunk at a Sunday School nativity play in my life and you know it. With or without a Donald Duck mask.

I shall not be sleeping anything whatsoever off on Thursday morning. I shall be dressing the Christmas tree on Thursday morning. Yes, *and* blowing up the balloons. *And* putting up the decorations. *And* checking the fairy-lights. *And* filling the stockings. *And* sending off the Christmas cards.

Of course it won't be too late! There is absolutely nothing wrong with leaving things until the last minute provided you know what you're doing.

Anyway, there's oceans of time yet. A whole week.

Yes, I *do* realise I've got a column to write. What do you think this is – a motto out of a Christmas cracker?

Grandad's Last Post

My old grandad would have got hot and bothered over the postal strike. He liked getting letters and he liked sending letters, although he could neither read nor write.

He was over ninety years old and he lived alone in a little mining village in Derbyshire. His married daughter, my mother, lived in Leeds.

She couldn't get down to see him all that often and it was pointless writing because there was no one to read her letters to him, and he wouldn't have cared to show them to anyone who wasn't family.

So they worked out between them a unique way of keeping in touch.

Every Monday morning my mother used to sit down at the kitchen table with the Stephen's ink-bottle and the Basildon Bond. As if it were the most important job in the world she would carefully address an envelope to herself.

Then she would stamp it, fold it in two and place it inside another envelope which she addressed to Grandad.

She caught the first post every week.

His Majesty's mails being a bit more reliable in those days, the envelope always reached Grandad on the Tuesday.

The postwoman once told my mother he so much looked forward to receiving it that he would often walk to the end of the lane and wait for her coming.

He would open his letter on the spot, take out its enclosure and study it for several moments, as if it contained some message that only he could understand.

Then he would walk across to the village post office and dispatch his stamped addressed envelope back to Leeds.

It always arrived by the first post on Wednesday and, in this way, my mother knew that he was safe and well. She never bothered to open the envelope, for of course it contained nothing.

This ritual went on for several years.

Sometime after Grandad's 95th birthday, my mother noticed one Wednesday morning that the postman had walked past the gate. She ran after him to see if he had forgotten her but no – there was no letter from Grandad that week.

She put on her coat, took the next train to Chesterfield, caught the little bus to the village where he'd lived, and buried him.

The Beast Of Brighton

This week, by mutual consent, the Beast of Brighton and I decided to part company. You have heard of the Loch Ness Monster? The Beast of Brighton is its cousin, once removed.

It is a strange, malevolent creature with a wickerwork hide and sinews of bamboo. When you touch the brute it creaks menacingly and breathes out evil dust-clouds through lungs of raffia. When you leave it alone it just crouches there, brooding.

But every so often, in the stillness of the evening, it stirs angrily and lets out a sort of grating shriek, like the Bridge of Tay on the night it collapsed with the resultant loss of ninety souls.

The Beast of Brighton is, in melancholy fact, an Edwardian beach-chair – a bulbous, hooded monstrosity six feet high, three and a half feet deep and, at its broadest, four feet across.

Picture a gigantic avocado pear sliced down the middle, scooped out and equipped with the seating capacity of a steam tram. That's my baby.

At one time, milk-skinned seaside belles in striped one-piece bathing suits reclined within that cavernous basketwork womb to protect themselves from the harmful rays of the sun.

Then it fell on evil days and finished up in a junk shop. Then I saw it, and it was my turn to fall on evil days.

I bought it for twelve quid in the laughable belief that it would do something for the living room of my flat.

It took two experienced removal men to squeeze it through the front door, and reinforcements were called to get it up the stairs.

There are still mysterious scratches on the paintwork consistent with King Kong having dropped in for a bite of lunch.

It did something for the living room all right. The Beast of Brighton threw an immense shadow from wall to wall like Stonehenge on Midsummer's Day.

'No,' I said after a full three seconds appraisal. 'I don't think it really improves the living room. Let's try the hall, shall we?'

So we tried the hall. Push. Pull. Prod. Heave. Charge. Coax. Kick. Bash. Threaten.

It didn't do a lot for the hall, either. In fact, if the hall had been able to speak it would have said: 'It's either you or me, buster, and if it comes to it, I belong in the lease.'

'The bedroom?' I suggested. The men had arrived at the crack of dawn and they were already on overtime.

Swear. Sweat. Squeeze. Shove.

By nine o'clock, using every weapon we could lay our hands on including the coal-tongs, we had driven the Beast of Brighton into the bedroom and the removal men were saying they didn't have to do this for a living, there was always road-sweeping.

In the bedroom the Beast remained.

It has been there, creaking and groaning, for two years. If you can imagine sharing a billet with the Graf Zeppelin, mooning restlessly around its mooring post during the long windy nights, that is what it has been like.

I have never dared sit in it, for fear of being swallowed alive. If I have gone near it with tempting offerings such as a fortnight's laundry, it has growled ominously.

The shadow across my bed has grown bigger. Sometimes I have fancied that the Beast was expanding, imperceptibly, like a science-fiction marrow about to take over the world.

In the middle of the night when it was creaking and cursing to itself I got up and said: 'Look, you and I have come a long way together and so I can speak freely. Wouldn't you be happier on a bonfire?'

Creak.

The second-hand clothes dealer said he would be delighted to cart the Beast away for nothing, provided I got the flaming thing out into the street first.

So I called in some removal men. Not the first lot, who refused to come, but another lot. They stared at the Beast in some awe.

'We'll have to take the door off its hinges,' they said at last.

'You can pull the wall down for all I care,' I said. 'Just get it off the premises.'

I gave them the key and waltzed off singing happily to myself, secure in the belief that I had seen the last of the Beast of Brighton.

Needless to say, when I got home it was still there, looming belligerently in the corner and creaking with quiet indignation.

'We can't understand it,' the removal men said. 'How did it get here in the first place?'

I explained that it was a long story. 'What we thought was,

39

it must have been built here. Either that, or it was craned up through the window.'

'No,' I said. 'It got in through the door.'

'In that case,' they said, 'it must have bloody well grown.'

'I know,' I said. 'That's what's worrying me.' And from the bedroom there was a sort of smug creak, and a shadow fell across the threshold.

Does anyone want to take over a nice flat, part-furnished?

Fortifying The Forties

When the history of the Forties is written – and you may expect it to be written a hundred times over during the next few months – I hope someone will have a chapter to spare for the advertising of the period.

The fashions and the flicks and the songs of that frugal decade are all enjoying a tremendous vogue just now. The King's Road, Chelsea, has become an extension of Memory Lane and any day now the once-trendy cardboard gas-mask cover is bound to become the latest thing in handbags.

But I doubt whether the boys who are usually first aboard the bandwagon will get much extra mileage out of their own contribution to the Forties. The ad-men are always ingenious; but their once-only, never-to-be-repeated offering during this time of great shortages was unique.

It was not the hard sell or the soft sell. It was the non-sell. Copywriters, draughtsmen and slogan-smiths would have burned the midnight oil, if there had been any midnight oil, to persuade us not to use products that weren't in the shops anyway.

'Every tin of Mansion Polish must do the work of two,' ran a typical punchy message. 'So use sparingly and less frequently.'

'If you are in actual need of a new Wisdom, please ask for it,' the toothbrush kings urged their customers. 'But if your chemist cannot supply, don't blame him.'

'Rose's Lime Juice – scarcer than hot water bottles in the Western Desert!' was a successful Instant Persuader that must have trebled nonsales overnight. And who can doubt the tremendous unpulling power of 'Sorry! There's no Kraft Cheese now being made'?

We were told to cut our Mars Bars into slices to make them last longer, to do jack-knife exercises as a substitute for fruit salts, and to cease our insane longing for canned peas and dig the garden instead.

The commercials of the day were as snappy as any TV jingle and patriotic with it:

'Forward to Victory and normal supplies of Bassett's Original Liquorice Allsorts.' Venus looks down on a war-torn world turning at last to Peace and Reconstruction 'We hope before long to be able to offer again our wide choice of quality pencils . . .'

Meccano fought off competition with the challenging slogan: 'We regret that we cannot supply these famous toys today.' Standard Fireworks opted for the wistful touch: 'We shall remember the Fifth of November . . . one of these days.' Acme Wringers must have made advertising history with: 'You'll just have to borrow Mrs Mullins's . . .'

Many shrewd point-of-no-sale campaigns were launched with the result that the cash registers were silent all over England. Consider this one for milk chocolate:

'It is some time since Cadbury's had milk for their chocolate, and their supplies of Milk Chocolate are now exhausted.'

Or this one for marmalade:

'War conditions restrict supplies of bitter oranges, which prevents the manufacture of Golden Shred. A Robertson product. You can depend on it.'

Soap: 'Mother has taught Sheila that Pears Soap and clear water is the sure way for keeping that lovely complexion, and Preparing to be a Beautiful Lady. We regret that Pears Transparent Soap is in short supply just now.'

Bacon: 'For six years our food factories have been, and still are almost entirely engaged in producing Harris's Bacon, Sausages and Canned Meats for the Ministry of Food and Armed Forces.'

Viyella took a quarter-page in *Punch* to announce that anyone who thought he had bought one of their shirts recently must be the victim of a mirage. The same delusionary theme was pursued by Caley's:

'What's this? A young lady with a box of chocolates – and Caley Fortune Chocolates, too? Can't be. Caley's aren't making Fortune now . . .'

The war ended and a note of cautious optimism began to enter these hitherto profitless announcements: 'Fashion has come back and Courtaulds Rayons are coming back also, although,' it was thought prudent to add, 'they are not yet available.'

Then, gradually there was milk chocolate in the shops again, the bacon and bangers were demobbed, and you could ask for a shirt without them ringing for the men in the white coats. And before we knew what had hit us, we were all singing about Murraymints.

Time And Motion

Every Saturday morning I go to my local supermarket to do a bit of shopping. At the checking-out desk I always find myself waiting impatiently while the lady in front of me pays for her groceries.

It is not usually the same lady but it might just as well be, for the following pantomime inevitably ensues:

The assistant tots up the purchases, places them in a carrier bag, and tells the lady that that will be £2.59 if she pleases.

The lady comes out of a deep reverie and looks extremely startled, as if the idea of actually paying for the goods was a novel innovation just dreamed up by a grasping management.

She opens her handbag and peers into it cautiously. I get the impression that she expects to find a live snake curled up inside it.

She locates a purse. She closes the handbag and opens the purse. This too comes in for some scrutiny before she extracts three pound notes.

She hands the money to the assistant, closes the purse, opens the handbag, replaces the purse, and closes the handbag.

The assistant gives the lady her change.

The lady puts down the change and opens the handbag. Despite the fact that she had the damned thing in her fist only three seconds earlier, *she cannot find her purse.*

She places a compact, a bunch of keys and a comb-case on the counter. The purse comes to light. She puts the purse on the counter and replaces the other items.

She closes the handbag and picks up the purse. She opens the purse and puts the change in it. She closes the purse. She puts down the purse and opens the handbag. She puts the purse in the handbag and closes the handbag.

Transaction complete. All she has to do now is get her carrier bag on the floor, open her handbag, and take out her gloves. She closes her handbag . . .

Has anyone ever thought of trouser pockets for women?

Life With Father

Dad, dad, are you listening, dad? Why have you got your eyes closed, dad? Dad! Dad! Are you asleep, dad?

Not any more, son.

Dad, dad, have you read the paper, dad?

Yes, son. Why don't you go and play with your chemistry outfit? Blow something up, there's a good lad.

Dad, dad, have you seen this report by Professor E. E. LeMaster, Professor of Sociology at Wisconsin University?

I don't want to know about it, son. Get off my foot.

You ought to read it, dad. Dad? Dad! He's written this report called 'The Embattled Human Male'. He says that fathers are now suffering from chronic emotional malnutrition, and are struggling to maintain their self-image in the face of aggressive wife-mothers and powerful adolescents.

You're spitting again, son. Never spit when reading aloud.

But dad, dad, it's important, dad!

I'm sure it is, son. Incidentally, there is an apple-core on the mantelpiece. If there is still an apple-core on the mantelpiece when I wake up again, there are those among us who will not be getting any pocket money on Saturday.

Don't you want to know about the Professor's report, dad?

No, son. I've had a long day.

So have I, dad. Do you know what Old Baggypants had the cheek to say, just because I was eating Turkish Delight during Scripture?

The name of your headmaster, lad, is Mr Braithwaite. Never say Old Baggypants. Always say Mr Braithwaite.

'The employers, the wife, and the children all want part of the father's life. But who cares about him?'

That's a funny thing for Old Baggypants to say, isn't it?

Not Mr Braithwaite, dad. The Professor. This Professor E. E. LeMaster. He says you're love-starved, dad. Dad? Dad, you're snoring again!

I know I am, son. It is my privilege to snore. I have just worked a sixty-hour week to buy luxuries such as fruit so that you can leave apple-cores on the mantelpiece and orange peel in the lavatory. Snoring, you may be interested to know, is what keeps me from going insane.

There's always the telly, dad.

I don't wish to discuss the telly. In fact, if you don't turn that programme down, the telly is going out of the window.

The Professor agrees with you, dad. He says that if the father turns to television for relief, his ego will be additionally assaulted by programmes in which women and children consistently outwit the father.

Is there much more of this, son?

Yards and yards of it, dad. It's an official UNESCO report.

Will you tell me something, son? Why don't you read the Beano like other boys in your age group?

I thought you'd be interested, dad.

I am interested, son. Isn't it time you were in bed?

It's only seven o'clock, dad. Dad? Dad! You promised you were going to bring home some plastic cement and help me build that do-it-yourself model of the Mayflower you got me for Christmas.

Some other time, son.

But dad, it was Christmas 1968 when you bought me it. There's only 7,000 parts, if you don't count the rigging.

Mm.

Dad? Dad! Can you hear me, dad? Do you feel love-starved, dad? Dad!

Wha'? What's happened? What's going on? Is the house on fire?

It's only me, dad. I was just asking if you feel love-starved.

Have you woken me up just to ask me that, son?

But it's important, dad! This professor says that sons and daughters nowadays belong to a self-willed generation working out their own destinies, so the father feels unloved.

Mm.

So do you, dad? Dad!

What? Do I what, son?

44

Feel unloved, dad Dad? Dad! Do you feel unloved?

Son, you are the flesh of my loins and the jewel of my life, but if you wake me up just once more, so help me God, you are going to feel the back of my hand!

Festive Occasion

Much to my own surprise, I was quite sensible and responsible when it came to filling in my census form yesterday, although the temptation to slip in a few daft answers was always there.

Unlike practically everyone else, it would seem, I cherish the census as an invaluable feature of British life.

Not for what it may produce in the way of useless statistics, but for the opportunity it presents for a gala display of national bloodymindedness.

I don't think I've met a single person who wasn't hell-bent on sabotaging his census form to the best of his ability. Some people intended to be deliberately stupid; others favoured illegibility and blots; a third contingent of the awkward squad planned entering the name of the family cat.

I'm sure none of this had anything to do with the supposed threat to our privacy. It was our God-given right to play silly buggers that was threatened, and the nation responded magnificently.

I have filled in my own form accurately, and with love, to encourage the Registrar-General to keep this important festival of contrariness alive.

Such Were The Joys

The saddest news of the week-end, for me, was that it has become necessary to turn a Cambridgeshire meadow into a cowslip museum.

The limited liability companies who plough the fields and scatter the dichloro-diphenyl-trichloroethane on the land have done their work well.

The cowslip is on the verge of entering that biological resting-ground inhabited by the dodo, the brontosaurus and other of nature's freaks which have outgrown their uses.

Primula veris, it will be called in the history books – a relative of *primula vulgaris* or common primrose, which I suppose is also not as common as it used to be on Mothering Sundays long ago.

The idea in Cambridgeshire is to preserve this humble little flower as you would preserve a horse-drawn cab or the last steam engine, so that children of future generations might come and wander through the spring grass and say to each other: 'So this is what a cowslip meadow looked like.'

I don't expect they'll be allowed to pick a frail yellow posy and traipse it, dripping petals, back to the coach, and clutch it tightly all the way home, and deposit it, already wilting and half-strangled with love, in an old jam-jar. More sensible, perhaps, if they make drawings in their nature-books and colour them in later with felt-tip pens.

What a shame that so much of the magic of childhood should vanish in a puff of insecticide, and that children's joys, like cowslips, are in danger of extinction.

There must already be millions of kids who have never been blackberrying or fished for tiddlers, or held a buttercup under their chins to see if it reflects pure gold which means you like butter.

Do they still make daisy-chains, chase butterflies, look for cuckoo-spit, organise newt-races, climb trees, and limp home at sunset covered in bramble-scratches and elderberry juice?

If so, I never see them doing it and there are now large tracts of England where these innocent pursuits are as obsolete as dancing round the maypole. The bulldozers, as much as DDT and the rival attractions of the telly, have seen to that.

Do the kids know what they're missing? Do they know how to split a blade of grass to make a whistle, or what particular hedge-plant is supposed to taste like bread-and-cheese, or how to recognise a thrush's egg?

Although I was brought up in a city and never mastered the difference between hips and haws on the school nature walks, I got a great deal of delight from chasing or gathering or collecting things.

There were times in our neighbourhood when there was hardly a discarded matchbox that didn't contain a furry caterpillar and a shrivelled-up bit of cabbage leaf. There were seasons of the year when the Co-op dairyman was seriously inconvenienced by the number of his milk bottles that held bluebells or tadpoles.

At every gatepost, so it seems now, some tiny tot would be in close communion with a ladybird.

We had a cowslip meadow too, only five minutes' walk from the streets where I grew up. It's part of a housing estate now, and so are the bluebell woods and the orchard and the field with the horse in it.

The ladybirds have all flown away home.

I can't claim that we would have made good copy for 'The Archers' but armed with a jam-jar and a home-made fishing-rod we certainly got our share of the outdoor life, and it was never more than a tram-ride away.

The children who grew up after us don't commune with nature, they commute to it. They have to take a bus to the green belt and leave their picnic litter in the basket provided, or they go on a school expedition to the cowslip museum, or for all I know the conker reserve in Epping Forest.

I've no doubt they know more about the birds and the bees than we did, but what about the flowers? What about the daisy-chains, the bluebells in the milk-bottle, buttercups under the chin, and bunches of drooping primroses on Mothering Sunday, and what about the redundant cowslips?

Sad. So sad.

Bedtime Stories

As the only living Englishman who has not yet pronounced on sex education, I feel it is time I made my views known.

I am in favour of it. My tick goes in the box marked 'Yes'. I speak from experience.

Unlike the sixth Earl Fortescue, who learned the knack of hatching a prospective seventh Earl Fortescue via his observations of dogs and cats, I acquired my knowledge of the reproductive processes in the classroom.

It is true that no teacher was ever present at these seminars, but they were no less enlightening for that. Our instructor in the facts of life was a precocious skinhead called Bullock who, although he was uncouth, unwashed and almost totally illiterate, enjoyed the reputation of a midget Dr Martin Cole.

Bullock knew it all.

His brilliant series of lectures, which generally took place under a desk-lid during milk-break, told us as much as it was humanly possible to know about sex short of actually finding a girl and doing it.

Bullock warned us of the awful perils of venereal disease which is picked up from lavatory seats.

He counselled us to beware of contraceptives, it being well known that every twelfth one has a pin-prick in it.

Masturbation, we learned from Bullock, makes you go blind. Circumcision is an irrevocable bar to marriage. Girls with ginger pubic hair are all nymphomaniacs.

Any house with a red lampshade is a brothel. Any woman with a bandage round her ankle is in the life-sapping throes of menstruation.

There is only one position for sexual intercourse, and that is standing up in a shop doorway.

Women who are unfaithful to their husbands give birth to black babies. Virgins cannot conceive at the first attempt. Wet dreams are the cause of tuberculosis.

Peeing in the swimming bath causes the water to turn green for twelve cubic feet all round.

Bullock eventually made friends with a kind gentleman in a raincoat who used to give sweets away in the recreation ground public lavatory, and shortly after that he seemed to lose his sense of vocation. At any rate, the lectures ceased.

We were all very grateful to him, for without his advice and instruction we would have grown up in complete ignorance. Bullock was the only one who ever told us anything.

So perhaps you can see why I'm in favour of sex education in schools.

I'm Backing Britain

You may have read that Mr Peter Walker thinks the back gardens of Britain should be tidied up so as to present a happier vista from the railway lines.

I have only one small amendment to this otherwise excellent proposal. Insert the word 'not' after the word 'should'.

Leave the back gardens of Britain alone. The back gardens of Britain are beautiful.

The rabbit hutches, the hen-runs and the half-dug goldfish ponds of old England are part of a rich heritage.

The coils of hosepipe hanging on the wall, the rusting bicycles, the planks, bits of roofing felt and scraps of corrugated iron which the old man has been planning to knock up into a tool shed since 1946, are what this country is basically all about.

Travel on the Norwood line from London Bridge on a Sunday morning and you will see what Shakespeare was getting at when he spoke of this scepter'd isle, this other Eden, this happy breed of men.

In one back yard a perspiring ratepayer on his day off is sawing plywood with no apparent object save that of building up a great stockpile of sawn plywood.

In another, for reasons no less obscure, a man is meticulously painting a bus tyre in red enamel.

In a third, an entire family is industriously shifting a compost heap from north to south, while, in a fourth, the same operation progresses from south to north.

A fifth back garden is a miniature boatyard where a canoe is undergoing stress experiments from two babies and a dog.

A sixth, where the father of the house has taken a blow-lamp to a zinc bath, resembles a thriving engineering works. A seventh is dedicated to the care and maintenance of a small goat.

All the back doors are open to the sun, and the scent of Yorkshire pudding and roast beef mingles with the heady odour of paint, turpentine, wood-shavings, glue and boiling tar.

If they ever make a musical of *Exchange and Mart,* they should set it in an English back garden.

The overture would be the signature tune of 'Two-Way Family Favourites' scored for a thousand transistor radios, and a flight of racing pigeons would signal the grand finale – a spectacular transformation scene in which a whippet-run is constructed, before our very eyes, from a roll of Army-surplus wire netting.

To glimpse the back yards from the railway lines is to recognise that the England of H. G. Wells, Arnold Bennett and Priestley's 'Good Companions' is surprisingly still alive.

It is an England of dabbling and pottering and messing-about which the planners, the environment economists and the council housing committees have done their best to smash into the ground. With all their power it is a miracle that they have so far failed.

The back yards thrive as hardily as the nettles and dandelions that infest their unfinished rockeries and the brambles entwining the skeletons of grandiose but abandoned summer-houses.

I would not want it any other way and I suspect that when he has thought about it, neither would Mr Peter Walker.

Delayed In Transit

I will tell you a very curious thing about delivery vans. They are always breaking down.

I will tell you an even more curious thing about delivery vans. Although they are always breaking down, you never see a broken-down delivery van.

I have scoured London looking for one in this unfortunate condition. I have peered down back alleys in the hope that some commercial vehicle on the skids might be hiding its misery in some dark and oil-stained corner.

The conclusion I have come to is that delivery vans are robust, reliable, hale and hearty. The only circumstance in which they break down is when they are on their way to deliver something to me.

'Hello? Is that the Incompetent Furniture Company?'

'*At your service, sir.*'

'You promised to deliver a bookshelf this morning. It is now four o'clock in the afternoon and it hasn't arrived.'

'*I'm terribly sorry, sir, but the van broke down.*'

Another quirk of delivery vans is that there is no clock or dial or device known to mankind whereby the time taken by them to get from one place to another may be estimated.

'Hello? Is that the Diabolical Laundry Ltd.?'

'*Your wish is our command, sir.*'

'Can you let me know roughly what time your van will be in my area today?'

'*I'm afraid I can't tell you that, sir.*'

'Why not have a shot at it? Why not say: "This morning", or "this afternoon", or "sometime between now and Boxing Day"?'

'It's impossible to say, sir. The van has already left.'

The last but one peculiarity of delivery vans is that they throw off noxious fumes which incapacitate their drivers for days and sometimes weeks on end.

And the absolutely final peculiarity is that the drivers, after they have been smitten by this mysterious illness, have no recollection of it at all.

'Evening, squire. Parcel for you from Snail & Tortoise Ltd. Sign here.'

'Thanks very much. Glad you're on your feet again.'

'Come again, squire?'

'I rang your office to find out why this parcel didn't arrive last Tuesday when it was promised. They said all the drivers were off ill.'

'There's only one driver, squire, and I'm it. Never felt better in my life. Ta-ra.'

'Ta-ra.'

Rum old things, delivery vans.

Bring Back The Boiled Egg

Did you know that it is possible to set off from Piccadilly Circus and walk for half an hour in any direction without finding a popular eating house that will serve you with a boiled egg?

You can get scrambled egg served in a baked potato. You can get a fried egg served on top of a mini-steak. You can get a ham omelette or a mushroom omelette or a plain omelette. You can get hamburgers, savoury pancakes, waffles and hot dogs. But, except possibly at the Ritz and Claridge's, whose chefs will serve any dish that money can buy, the art of boiling eggs for public consumption is lost.

This might not strike you at first as the most earth-shattering news item you have ever read. But think. Britain was built on boiled eggs. Every home has its little nest of egg cups, often in the shape of a duck, pussy cat, dog or other homely animal. We go to work on an egg. We come home to an egg.

'Hey little hen,' we used to sing in the dark days of the war, 'when when when will you lay me an egg for my tea?' The demand is there. Where is the supply?

I'll tell you something else. It's almost as difficult to get hold of the traditional English snack of tea and piping hot toast. Perhaps there are still a few teashops in the provinces where maiden ladies preside over the pop-up toaster among the chintz and copper kettles. But in the West End of London the institution has almost disappeared.

I set out with a Belgian friend one day looking for tea and toast, which as an Anglophile he fancied. We finished up eating doughnuts at a plastic counter the width of the average window ledge.

Another thing: Yorkshire puddings. When I was a growing lad I used to go to a café that turned out Yorkshire pudding as it should be eaten – that is, the size of a dinner plate, served as an hors d'oeuvre before the meat and potatoes. That's how northerners eat their Yorkshire pudding at home, and that's how they liked it when they ate out. Not any more, apparently. The café still exists, but it has gone over to mini-steaks and beefburgers.

You used to hear a lot about the 'eating revolution', one of the many social upheavals that are supposed to have convulsed Britain since the war. Broadly speaking, it's reckoned by those who cover the good food front to have been an admirable thing. English restaurants were traditionally so foul that any Italian, Greek or Indian who did not actively give his customers ptomaine poisoning could not help but make money.

But there's been another 'eating revolution' too, a less successful one, and that's in the field of what you could call utility eating. Most people who eat out in this country don't do so for social purposes. They're either snatching a quick bite during the lunch hour or grabbing an early supper before going to the pictures. All they want is cheap food, good service and pleasant, hygienic surroundings.

If you ate yesterday at one of the old-fashioned popular cafés you probably had to queue up at a counter with a battered metal tray to collect a meal that was congealed before you had even paid for it. You then had to share a plastic table with several other people, and you would be very lucky if one of them wasn't a crazed old man who was rolling cigarettes and muttering to himself about some grievance he had against Somerset House.

Rightly enough, these institutions have been challenged in recent years by a new kind of pop restaurant. It is, in theory, clean, bright and efficient. You can, in theory, be in and out of the premises in twenty minutes having, in theory, fed simply but well at a reasonable cost.

I must say that every time I've ventured into one of these places I've found that what works on paper doesn't work in practice. I had lunch in one yesterday.

Although it was geared to serve hundreds of people every hour it seemed to have no system for clearing up after them, so that you had the sensation of dining inside a vast, brilliantly-lit dustbin.

Although there must have been at least £5,000-worth of refrigeration equipment on view, the so-called 'cold drinks' were served lukewarm from a display shelf. Quite ordinary requests, as it might be for a glass of water, were met with open hostility.

But what struck me most – as it always does – was the impossibility of getting anything that I really wanted to eat. The menu was simple to the point of feeble-mindedness. There were literally not more than six main dishes to choose from, and none of these was what you could call English food in any kind of English tradition. And when I had finished eating – standing at a counter, with my arms pinioned between two other diners – I was still ravenously hungry.

Now there is a general notion, largely put about by the people who run them, that eating houses of this kind are run on American lines, the implication being that the pace of life is getting more hectic by the hour and that this is the only way we can live it. This theory, too, is an erroneous one and I will tell you why.

It's true that the hamburgers, doughnuts, waffles, pancakes and whatnot that sizzle on a thousand English hotplates are American orientated, but there the resemblance stops. We have imported the substance but not the spirit of American eating.

In any American town, even one the size of Slough, you will find at least one coffee-shop that is spacious, spotless, and very probably open 24 hours a day.

You sit in comfortable booths and are served by pleasant waitresses who have already cleared away the debris from any previous occupant. You are given a menu the size of a pillow-case, and you may choose from as many as thirty or forty hot dishes.

You can have breakfast at four in the afternoon, if you wish, or you can have a three-course dinner at six in the morning. And the menu consists exclusively of the food that Americans actually like to eat, rather than something that has been invented for them in the interests of rapid turnover, limited cooking facilities or the highest possible profit.

I have never yet found a popular restaurant anywhere in Britain that could match one of these establishments, which ordinary American workers take as their right and due.

The reason is a very simple one. American coffee shops set off with the object of fulfilling a need. The English set off to create a demand. And the sad thing is that, perhaps, in the end they were right. The hamburger has become a national dish at last, and we had nothing at all to lose except our boiled eggs, our tea and toast, and our Yorkshire puddings.

Where Did Spring Go?

There are always more bad statistics than good statistics around, and among this week-end's depressing batch is one about abortions among teenagers.

They're going up, naturally. (You wouldn't expect them to be going down in this day and age, would you?)

Five hundred and forty-four of them were carried out on girls under sixteen, in the last three months of 1970, compared with 386 in the last three months of 1969. Better than pushing 544 prams to school, I suppose, but still gloomy tidings.

Everyone knows that children grow up quicker than forced rhubarb these days. Even using a word like 'teenagers' makes me feel about ninety years old.

It seems to belong with bobby-socks and Judy Garland musicals.

What are you supposed to call them now – I mean if you want to be polite? Young people? Kids? Junior citizens? Senior citizens?

Whatever name they go under it seems to me a shame that

they've had to bypass spring in their headlong flight towards the joys (and some of the tears) of summer.

Out of the cradle and into the bed is a spectacular jump, but aren't they losing something – besides their virginity, I mean – on the way?

I wonder what happened to calf love? And schoolgirl crushes? And schoolboy crushes, if it comes to that? And letters with SWALK (for Sealed with A Loving Kiss) or BOLTOP (Better On Lips Than On Paper) on the flap? And blind dates? And the back row of the pictures?

They don't even write love poems any more. They write poems about the environment of Stepney.

Am I being hopelessly sentimental in thinking that there was a magic in the first kiss which is not quite equalled by its present-day equivalent of the first grope?

Or that it was exciting enough just wondering whether she'd even turn up – let alone whether you'd finish the night on her mattress?

When teenagers really were called teenagers it was considered the fashion to carry a contraceptive in your wallet; the only difference between then and now being that it never got used.

You hunted in pairs and, if you had my luck, you always finished up with the ugly one.

It was your privilege to pay for the cinema tickets and, if you could get your arm around her before the end of British Movietone News, you were in clover.

Future dates were negotiated via an elaborate diplomatic network involving her friend and your friend.

Thereafter it was usual to go Dutch. Going Dutch did *not* mean having a fitting at the local family planning clinic.

It's all as old-hat as the foxtrot now, and adolescence, which used to be a way of life, has become purely a medical term to account for spots. At the age of ten, yet!

I still think there was a lot to be said for growing up at slightly less than the speed of sound.

Having your hand slapped off a lisle-covered kneecap may have been frustrating – but at least the only thing your girlfriend worried about missing was the last bus home.

Day Of The Dogsbody

As well as being a practising columnist I am honorary president, chairman, secretary, treasurer, organiser and chief bottlewasher of a small dog preservation society.

The latter appointments take precedence over the former.

The small dog in question is a humdrum Norwich terrier which answers to the name of Brandy – or, rather, refuses to answer to the name of Brandy – and he is the thickest animal to walk this earth since the pea-brained brontosaurus.

The founder-members of the society are three children who disagree with their hon. president's assessment of this hound's IQ. According to them he is alert and bright and such an intellectual among dogs that if only he could have got his paws round a typewriter he would have written 'War and Peace'.

The Small Dog Preservation Society meets on Sunday mornings and I forgot to mention that I am also the social secretary. In this capacity I arrange that the dog Brandy should go walkies.

In his capacity of canine village idiot, the dog Brandy arranges that while on these walkies he should get lost.

Not always. Not invariably. Sometimes he gets his head stuck in a rabbit-hole and on one occasion he was marooned up a tree. But getting lost is his speciality.

The minutes of the SDPS record that we arrived in the park at 10.30 a.m. and that by 10.32 a.m. our dumb chum had vanished without trace.

When last seen he was wearing a dopey expression and was engaged in one of his favourite hobbies, which is paddling on the edge of the pond. He has to paddle on the edge of the pond because he is the only dog in Great Britain that can't swim.

A trail of wet pawprints led into thin air.

The Society's representatives began to call his name. They began to call several other names too, for experience has shown that if he is going to come at all he will respond to any monicker from Archibald to Zebedee.

An hour passed. Various small dogs were spotted on the far horizon, pursued, caught, lined up for identification and rejected. The park seemed to be teeming with small dogs, all of them fast on their feet.

The founder-members of the Small Dog Preservation Society split up and began to search in different directions. The park is a very large one and it soon began to dawn on the hon. president that the strength had been reduced not only by a dog but also by three children.

It was now noon, by which time this column is supposed to be simmering under a low light, and I reckon on assembling my thoughts in re the Common Market, Leeds United, the poverty of the Queen and the indiscretions of Mr James Prior.

Instead of that I was stumbling through the bracken asking people if they had seen three children without a small dog or alternatively a small dog without three children.

By one o'clock the founder-members of the Society had re-convened. The minutes record that they listened attentively to a short informal lecture by their hon. president.

The search continued.

The police were informed. The park rangers were informed. There was some brisk telephone work in the course of which a lunch appointment was cancelled and the *Mirror* was asked to brick up this space until further notice.

The whole park was by now in a state of turmoil. Total strangers were rounding up small dogs and presenting them for inspection. A policeman on a motor-bike reported that an animal answering the accused's description had nipped a lady on the ankle.

A park ranger galloped by in pursuit of what turned out to be a ginger cat.

At 3 p.m. the founder-members and president of the SDPS trooped back, for the umpteenth time, to the spot where the vanishing trick had taken place.

The dog Brandy was sitting at the edge of the pond crying softly to himself, snapping at sympathisers and waiting with some impatience for the meeting to resume. He had been AWOL for four-and-a-half hours.

Tearful reunion. Two minutes later the entire incident was expunged from his tiny mind for ever and he was trying to run away again.

The founder-members of the SDPS voted unanimously that happiness is finding a lost dog.

The hon. president moved an amendment: that happiness is booting a dog from here to Timbuctoo. The meeting was adjourned.

Blanket Coverage

The Post Office, for about the tenth time, has sent me instructions on how to use the Postcode.

Under the heading 'Correct method of showing the Postcode in an address', I am told to observe the following rules:

'1. Always show the Postcode as the last item of the address. 2. Always write the Postcode in block capitals. 3. Do not use full stops or other punctuation marks anywhere in the Postcode. 4. Leave a clear space, equivalent to at least one character, between the two parts of the Postcode.'

And so on, down to rule 13: 'LONDON should always be shown in the address even for correspondence posted in London.'

All day yesterday I was trying to remember what this meticulous nonsense put me in mind of. It's just hit me.

When I was doing my National Service we had a sergeant who made a fetish of properly-folded blankets. However neatly we stacked them on our beds he was never satisfied. He spent all his free time writing notices entitled: 'Correct method of folding blankets'.

I can still recall some of his rules. '1. Blankets will be folded to a depth of 1¾ inches. 2. Sheets will be folded to a depth of one-third of an inch. 3. Thin blankets which sag when folded will be returned to stores.'

I'd often wondered what happened to that blankety sergeant. Clearly, he's working for the Post Office in London W1P 1AA.

The Parents' Charter

A couple of kids stopped me in Oxford Street and sold me, for five pence, a smudgy copy of the Charter of Children's Rights.

They'd run it off on a duplicator in flagrant breach, I suspect, of the original copyright.

Anyway, full marks for initiative. And full marks, too, to the Children's Charter which – although this particular copy of it was practically indecipherable – I happen to know is full of good sense.

'Children have the right to privacy of person and thought . . .

to freedom of expression . . . to freedom from political indoc-
trination . . .

'A child's personal appearance is his own and his family's
concern . . . Children have the right to such knowledge as is
necessary to understand the society in which they live . . . They
shall have the freedom to make complaints about teachers and
parents without fear of reprisal . . .'

Fine. Agreed. Accepted. Right on.

But, dear children, has it ever occurred to you that parents
have their rights too? I would be very surprised if this revolutionary thought has ever entered your heads, and for that reason,
I have drafted, for your consideration, a Charter of Parents'
Rights.

Run it off on your duplicator by all means but don't try to
sell it to me. Sell it to each other.

1. Parents have the right to their sleep. If you've promised
to be in by 10.30 they have no wish to be counting the flowers
on the wallpaper at one in the morning.

2. Parents have the right to freedom from unnecessary worry.
If it takes you three hours to nip out and buy an iced lolly it
will not occur to your parents that half-way down the road you
decided to go to a pop concert instead. They will conclude that
you have been raped, kidnapped or murdered, or a grisly com-
bination of all three.

3. A parent's personal appearance is his own concern. He does
not want to be told that his hair is too short or that turn-ups
are out of fashion. Nor does he require a psychedelic kipper tie
on Father's Day.

4. Parents have the right to be human beings. That is to say,
they have the right to fall into irrational rages, to contradict
themselves, to change their minds without reason, to be stubborn, dogmatic and bloodyminded, and in general to behave
occasionally like children, who as you well know are the salt of
the earth.

5. No parent shall be scoffed at, sneered at or in any way
discriminated against for his opinions. If a parent takes the view
that the popular ballad, 'Leap up and down, wave your knickers
in the air' is not the greatest song since 'Greensleeves', that is
entirely his own affair.

6. Parents have the right to freedom from political indoctrina-
tion. It may well be the case that the world would be perfect if

all money were distributed equally, the police force abolished, pot legalised, and the factories turned into communes, but your parents are not necessarily shambling morons if they prefer to go on voting Co-op-Labour.

7. Parents have the right to the enjoyment of their own home. They are unlikely to enjoy their own home if one of the bedrooms appears to have been converted, without planning permission, into an indoor piggery. You may argue that your room is nothing to do with them. A glance at the rentbook will prove otherwise.

8. Parents shall have the freedom to make complaints about their children without fear of reprisal. The expression 'reprisal' includes sulking, screaming, slamming doors, making a motion with the hand as if winding up a gramophone, and threatening to throw yourself in the river.

9. All parents shall have the right to expect a reasonable return for their labour. Having acted, over the years, as your unpaid nurse, teacher, cook, cleaner, nightwatchman, swimming instructor, banker, valet, hairdresser, boot-black, launderer, odd-job man and general dogsbody, they are surely entitled to ask you to fill the coal bucket once in a while.

10. Parents have the right to such knowledge as is necessary for them to understand the society in which they live. This means that they should be told exactly why you have painted the words 'Screw the Pigs' in four-foot letters across the garage doors, what this inscription means, and how you propose to erase it.

11. Parents shall not be humiliated because of their own inadequacies. They shall not be addressed in O-level French, grilled on the subject of the principal rivers of Australia, or be required to make head or tail of the New Mathematics. At public dances, parents have the right to foxtrot without being mocked.

12. Parents shall have the inalienable freedom to nag, criticise, threaten, cajole, warn, scold, and offer gratuitous advice. They carry on in this boring way not because they enjoy it but because they have a duty to exercise their most precious right of all which is:

13. Parents have the right to be parents.

Call Of The Wild

All I wanted was to make a desperately urgent phone call to a village in Suffolk. You couldn't dial it direct. You had to go through the operator.

Only the trouble was, I couldn't reach the operator. Whenever I dialled 100, all I got was a sort of dead click.

The phone book tells you what to do on such occasions. For difficulties on dialled calls, it says, dial 100.

It doesn't say what you should do when you have difficulty in dialling 100.

I had to use my own initiative. I browsed among the available numbers – 192 (Directory Enquiries), 190 (Ships' Telegrams), and 246 8047 (Main Events of the Day in Spanish).

I settled for 151 (Telephone Out of Order or Broken).

Bzz-bzz, bzz-bzz.

'Engineers. If you're reporting a fault, there'll be nobody here until eight in the morning.'

'Yes, but ——.'

Click. Bzzzzz. There were no buts to be butted, for 151 had hung up.

I dialled again, with the intention of having a word with 151 on the subject of good manners.

Bzz-bzz, bzz-bzz.

Different voice this time. Female. Polite.

'Engineers here. Can I help you?'

'Oh, good evening. Listen, can you tell me how to get in touch with the operator when ——.'

'Dial 100 for the operator.'

'Yes, I know, but the whole point is ——.'

Click. Bzzzzzz.

I crossed 151 off my list and transferred my affections to 191 (Other Telephone Enquiries).

Bzz-bzz, bzz-bzz.

'Can I help you?'

'I sincerely hope so. I've been trying to get the operator and ——. '

'Dial 100.'

'Yes, I know all about that, but if you'll just let me finish my ——.'

'If you want the operator, dial 100 and wait.'

'—— sentence, what I'm trying to tell you is ——.'

'*What's your number?*'

'—— that I've already tried to ——.'

'*What's your number?*'

'—— dial the operator, and all that happens is ——.'

'*What's your number?*'

'—— that I get a sort of clicking noise.'

'I know that already. What's your number?'

'You can't possibly have known that already, because I've only just finished telling you. My number is ——.'

Click. Bzzzzzz.

A couple of blazing quarrels later, someone told me to dial 198. This is an unlisted number which is probably reserved for dealing with loonies.

Bzz-bzz, bzz-bzz.

'Yes?' snapped the surliest voice imaginable.

'Good evening. I was told that you could put me in touch with the op——.'

'*What do you want?*'

'I want a telephone number. What the hell do you think I want – a toasted teacake?'

To cut a long case of the screaming habdabs short, 198 finally got me the operator and the operator finally got me my number.

Bzz-bzz, bzz-bzz.

'Oh, there you are,' said my friend in Suffolk. 'I've been trying to ring you for the last twenty minutes, but you were engaged.'

Plumbing The Depths

I have this problem. My bath tap, when turned full on, operates at only half force. When turned half on, it doesn't work at all. When turned off again, it will not work for a full hour.

I am sure there is a very simple explanation for this and that all it needs is a washer or a good swift kick.

So if anyone can tell me, preferably with the aid of simple diagrams, (*a*) how to get the casing off my bath tap and (*b*) what to do when I've got it off, I'll be grateful.

And if these lines are read by the plumber who was supposed

to turn up at 9.30 one morning last week, may he stew in hell.

My way of life is a simple one and during the last six months I've needed outside help on only four occasions. I wanted a decorator to wallpaper the kitchen, an odd-job man to do the sash cords, an electrician to do something about some sparks, and a plumber to fix the bath tap.

Of these four, only the electrician turned up when he was supposed to, and the bill, due to a computer error, was for £470.

The sash cord man never arrived at all, and as for the decorator, he came five days late and took a fortnight over an estimated thirty-six hours work.

He used to leave hysterical notes for me on bits of wallpaper, describing the twists of fate that prevented him finishing the job – the wholesalers had let him down, his van had been stolen, his employers had given him the wrong address.

Daily, I expected to find my kitchen wall scrawled with a denunciation of some Zionist plot against him. A man with a persecution complex, my decorator.

The plumber – or plumbers, I should say, as there were seven of them – are in a class of their own.

Four of them refused to come at all. The fifth thought he could make it by 10 a.m. but seemingly felt unable to meet the challenge. The sixth promised on his mother's grave to come at 8.30 the next morning and left a card saying: 'Called at 4 p.m. – no reply'.

The seventh plumber was recommended by friends, who swore affidavits as to his reliability. I had three careful telephone calls with him, when he promised, reiterated and confirmed that he would be on my premises, tool bag at the ready, at 9.30 a.m.

I don't have to tell you that he didn't arrive. I missed two appointments and at 1 o'clock, in a blind rage, rang him up. The following conversation, I swear, is true.

Plumber: 'But I've been ringing your office since 11 o'clock to tell you I was on my way and there was no reply.'

Me: 'Naturally there was no reply from my office, because I've been here waiting for you.'

Plumber: 'Oh. I should have thought of that, shouldn't I?'

Of course, these adventures are not isolated. Everyone I know has an anecdote about the gasmen who arrived six days late to search out a leak, or the Electricity Board sending forty-seven men and three vans to change a screw in a light socket.

Now the worst aspect of discussing this sort of thing is that if you're not careful you're likely to find yourself on the same side as the purple old Tories, and the next thing you know is you're being asked to sign a petition to restore corporal punishment for trade unionists.

Happily, it's fairly easy to hold out. If there is a social reason for ineptitude on its present scale, it's that more and more people can afford to have things done for them and so the waiting lists get longer.

In any case, I should mention that with the single exception of the clown on the telephone, all my seven plumbers were not inefficient workmen but inefficient firms, and very big firms at that.

There must be some deep-seated reason for it all. Whether it's historical, geographical, meteorological or what I don't pretend to know.

The only thing I am sure of is that, along with management reform, industrial reform and all the rest of it, what England really needs is a psychiatrist.

And meanwhile, back at the bath tap, what I need is a plumber.

Keep Taking The Tablets

Dear Dr Waterhouse, I write a column in a daily newspaper, and all week long I worry about what I am going to write about next. Can this give me an ulcer?

Of course it can, you mad, irresponsible fool. In fact it sounds to me as if you've got one already. In heaven's name see your doctor at once.

Although I have told my doctor that I think I am getting an ulcer, he merely chuckles and says I am neurotic. What is your opinion?

It would not be ethical for me to criticise a colleague, but clearly this man should be arraigned before the General Medical Council and pelted with stones. Have no further truck with him. Go to your chemist's and buy some glucose tablets. These will clear up your ulcer.

Nearly every night, when I am about to drop off to sleep, my right foot gives a sort of involuntary jump, and I have the sensation of falling through space. Is this anything to worry about?

Funny you should ask that, because I suffer from the same thing myself. You should worry about it, yes. It sounds like a premonition that you're going to die in your sleep. Please write and let me know if this happens.

My gums sometimes bleed slightly when I brush vigorously. Does this mean that all my teeth are about to drop out?

Unfortunately, it does. Strictly speaking, of course, this is a problem for your dentist. But I beg you, whatever you do, not to go near him, otherwise he will pull all your teeth out.

Two friends of mine have recently suffered mild heart attacks. Does this mean I am about to get one too?

Almost certainly. Next question.

Whenever my friends get flu they make light of it, as if it were merely a nuisance. When I get flu, however, I think I am about to die. Why is this?

There are many different kinds of flu. Clearly you suffer from what we call Serious Flu. This is a killer disease for which the only known cure is a week in bed.

I am a little overweight and am beginning to think it's time I started some exercise. Do you think this is a good idea?

How old are you? Forty-two? I thought so. You do not need to start worrying about taking exercise just yet. The only reason you are overweight is because you eat too much bread. You could start cutting down on this, say, next month.

I'm afraid I disregarded your advice about exercise and did some press-ups. Now I have a pain in both my arms. Am I worrying unduly about this?

I'm not too sure. There's an outside chance, of course, that the pain is merely muscular. On the other hand, it could be the symptom of something quite dreadful. I should spend an hour with the medical dictionary if I were you.

According to the medical dictionary, I seem to have all the early symptoms of an unmentionable disease. How can I set my mind at rest?

You do not mention what unmentionable disease you have the early symptoms of. If it is leprosy (p. 107), you will find that the symptoms will clear up when you discover you have yellow fever (p. 604).

Whenever I have stayed up smoking and drinking until 3 a.m.,

I wake up with a severe headache. Is there a connection?

None whatsoever. Severe headaches are caused by going to sleep in a stuffy room. Throw up the window before going to bed.

Last night I threw up the window before going to bed, and nearly fell out of it. Am I drinking too much?

Not if you can take it or leave it alone, which I'm sure you can. When you start cutting down on bread next month, try cutting down on booze also.

I am very short of breath. What can I do?

I know what you can't do, and that's run up four flights of stairs. We're all short of breath, for God's sake. Stop moaning and make do with the breath you have.

Yes, but I get these pains in my side when I run after a bus. Isn't that a symptom of something?

If God had meant you to run after buses he'd have given you spiked shoes. The time to start worrying about pains in your side is when you get them without stirring out of your armchair.

I do.

Oh. Well in that case, it's appendicitis.

I have read that people who think they have only got appendicitis are in fact suffering from goodness-knows-what chronic ailment. Is it too early to throw myself in the river?

Difficult to say. After all, you're forty-two years old and you've never had a day's illness in your life, so possibly you're destined for a ripe old age. On the other hand, perhaps your luck's running out. Why don't you take some more glucose tablets and, if the trouble doesn't clear up, throw yourself in the river?

I am a hypochondriac. Is there anything I can do about this?

Yes. Start a club, and I'll join it.

The Appetizer

It's curious how the magic names of childhood keep cropping up in the City pages – Meccano, Dinky Toys, BSA, and now Tizer, which is the subject of a great take-over deal.

Awesome news, that. When the pop man used to come down our street on Sunday mornings, with his horse-drawn cart piled high with crates of lemonade and dandelion and burdock, we always thought he made Tizer himself, brewing it in his kitchen from the cornucopia of luscious fruits that was illustrated on the label.

You can keep your Pepsi Generation. We came alive with the Tizer Generation. Those odd-shaped bottles – forty years ahead of the Post Office Tower in their functional design, and perfect for clutching in two small fists while you took a deep swig – accompanied us everywhere.

No fishing expedition was complete without a supply of Tizer when you dunked the bottle in the corporation reservoir to keep it cool. When it was empty you had a useful receptacle for tadpoles, and when the tadpoles were dead you could get a penny back on the bottle.

In our group, Tizer was regarded as common property to be passed around like a loving-cup. Cads and bounders would pretend to spit in the bottle before passing it on, greedy-gutses would guzzle half the bottle and thus be barred from further communion, and a true friend was one who didn't bother to wipe the neck with his sleeve before taking his turn.

Tizer belongs with the liquorice bootlace, the sherbet dab, the lucky bag and the all-day sucker as a classic among the good things of life. Long may it continue to be The Appetizer.

Any Excuse

A man I know in the building game swears that this is true. His boss, having ordered some plastic tiles on the fifth ult, or whenever it might be, wrote to ask why they were not forthcoming.

He got this reply:

'We regret the delay in expediting your esteemed order. Due to redundancies in our packing department, we are at present short of staff . . .'

Silent Nights

Where have all the carol-singers gone? I haven't heard one this year except for the Sally Army who don't really count because they're professionals working in an essentially amateur field.

An urchin of my acquaintance tells me that the bottom has dropped out of the market. He blames the telly – either people don't hear the raucous chorus of 'Once in Royal David's City' or they can't be bothered coming to the door.

I must say that in my own carol-singing days we would have needed stiffer rivals than Morecambe and Wise or the Trouble-shooters. We *were* the Troubleshooters. If the clients wouldn't come to the door we simply went on hammering until they did, and if they hadn't heard the token rendering of 'Good King Wenceslas knocked a bobby senseless, right in the middle of Marks and Spencers', it was their bad luck.

Sometimes they'd switch off the living-room lights and hide in the kitchen. This did them no good at all. We would simply switch the offensive to the back door and shatter their eardrums with a lusty reprise – or do I mean reprisal? – of:

While shepherds watched their turnip tops,
A-boiling in the pot,
An Angel of the Lord came down,
And scoffed the blinking lot.

When they realised the house was surrounded they'd come out with their hands up, to find themselves confronted by the juvenile equivalent of the Mafia. If they had no dog to set on us, they'd have to listen while we piped up our seasonal greeting:
'*A little bit of spice cake, a little bit of cheese, a glass of cold water, a penny if you please. If you haven't got a penny, a halfpenny will do, if you haven't got a halfpenny, you door's going through.*'
They knew that we meant it and coughed up accordingly.

Getting In Line

A White Paper published yesterday announces radical changes in the English language.

The Government's proposals are complex and far-reaching, but in effect they mean that in five years' time we will all be speaking Japanese.

The White Paper says: 'The Government has no wish to discourage the use of English conversation in pubs and at street corners, at least for the time being.

'For commercial transactions, however, the present obsolete, ramshackle vocabulary will gradually be phased out and replaced by Japanese.'

The chairman of the newly-formed Language Board explained: 'For many years the Japs have been leaping ahead of us in production, productivity and sheer commercial know-how. A decade from now they will have the highest standard of living in the world.

'How can we hope to keep up with our competitors if we do not even speak the same language?'

He added that speaking Japanese has been legal in this country for many years. The only reason the English had continued to use their native tongue was that they were stubborn, insular, old-fashioned and pig-ignorant.

The chairman of one of Britain's largest manufacturing groups welcomed the changes yesterday.

'If we are to keep our place in the world, and if I am to get a new Rolls-Bentley every year,' he said, 'it is essential to keep on messing about with ordinary people's lives.

'They stood for decimalisation without a whimper, and there's not much fuss about metrication, so by the time we start rounding up prices in Japanese they should be pretty well house-trained.'

A spokesman for industry said: 'The changeover will present many difficulties, but we have got to think of this in terms of my new swimming pool. Switching to Japanese may cause some initial confusion but it will mean that we can double our profits without anyone noticing except the customer.'

There was marked enthusiasm in the City, where a leading financier said: 'At board-room level, there has always been great difficulty in pronouncing the letter "r". Bringing English into line with Japanese will streamline our business discussions with the result that we shall get home in time for afternoon tea.'

The White Paper concedes that some people are so un-educated that they cannot even speak English properly, let alone Japanese. For their benefit all price labels and direction signs will appear in both languages for at least a fortnight.

The chairman of the Language Board said: 'We are acutely conscious that old-age pensioners, in particular, may experience some bewilderment at having to speak Japanese. However, if they do not like it they can always commit hara-kiri.'

Pressing Problems

The directors of the Diabolical Steam Laundry Ltd. have been holding their customary annual meeting to decide how they can best persecute Waterhouse during the coming year.

'Despite an initial setback when we almost returned Mr Waterhouse's laundry intact on two successive occasions, this was an excellent year for our company,' reported the chairman.

'At least a dozen of Mr Waterhouse's shirts were lost without trace during the period under review. We were successful in making large holes in Mr Waterhouse's pillow-cases.

'On one occasion we were able to mislay his entire laundry for a whole month, and I need not remind the Board of our un-precedented achievement in sending him several pairs of frilly pink knickers in mistake for his underpants.

'However,' the chairman warned, 'the Diabolical Steam Laundry cannot rest on its laurels. To stand still in our business is to go backwards. If we are to keep abreast of our competitors, we must be even more diabolical to Mr Waterhouse in the diffi-cult days ahead.'

The Director in charge of Shredding Operations was the first to make a suggestion. 'I'm just thinking aloud,' he said, 'but supposing we rip one of his sheets in half and send it back to him as a pair?'

'That trick was old when I was a junior towel-starcher,' said the chairman testily. 'Give me something the other laundries aren't doing already.'

The Director with Special Responsibility towards Shrinking

said: 'I'm just running this up the flagpole to see if it salutes, but how about shrinking all his shirts?'

The chairman looked at him coldly. 'I would have thought,' he retorted, 'that you were already doing that as a matter of course. In any case, if we had applied ourselves with the proper zeal during the year, Mr Waterhouse would no longer have any shirts left to shrink. Let's hear what the Scorch Marks and Dirty Footprints Department have to offer.'

'We're planning a new laundry box that will fall apart as soon as he picks it up off the doorstep,' said the Dirty Footprints Controller. 'The only snag is, I can't guarantee that it will always fall into a puddle.'

'Keep working on it,' said the chairman. 'Any more ideas?'

'I'm just pushing this off the end of the pier to see if it floats,' mused the Manager of the Frayed Collars Division, 'but why don't we slip a few drops of dye into the fraying machine so that all his laundry comes out mottled pink?'

'If you spent more time doing your job and less time chatting up the girls in the Button-snipping Department,' observed the chairman nastily, 'you would know that all Mr Waterhouse's laundry has been mottled pink since 1969. Anyone else?'

The managing director, a thoughtful, military-looking man who had had a distinguished career in psychological warfare, pulled shrewdly at his pipe.

'I'm just plugging this into the socket to see if it lights up,' he said. 'But supposing, one week, we just send Waterhouse's laundry back on the right day, at the right time, all nicely starched and pressed, and with not so much as a handkerchief missing?'

'I don't get it,' said the chairman. 'What would be the point of that?'

'Well, it'd get him worried. He'd wonder what the hell we were up to.'

'That's the lousiest idea I've ever heard,' said the chairman, glancing at his watch. 'All right, everybody, it's time to go out and kick Mr Waterhouse's laundry round the coke compound for half an hour. But I want you all back in the board room at two o'clock with some brand new diabolical wheezes.'

'Ah, well,' said someone. 'Back to the old ironing board.'

'I heard that,' snarled the chairman. 'Any ironing in *this* organisation, and you're fired.'

71

Albert And The Liner

Below the military striking clock in the City Arcade there was, and probably still is, a fabulous toyshop.

Once a year we were taken to see the clock strike noon, and after the mechanical soldiers of the King had trundled back into their garrison, we were allowed to press our noses to the toyshop window.

Following a suitable period of meditation, we were then supposed to compose our petitions to Father Christmas.

The centrepiece of the fabulous toyshop's window display was always something exotic such as the Blackpool Tower in Meccano, or a twin-track Hornby train running over a viaduct. None of us had to be told that such luxuries were beyond Father Christmas's price-range.

This year the window featured a splendid model of the Queen Mary, which had recently been launched on Clydebank. It was about four feet long, with real lights in the portholes and real steam wisping out of the funnels, and clearly it was not for the likes of us.

Having seen it and marvelled at it, we dismissed this expensive dream from our minds and settled down to list our prosaic requests for Plasticine, farmyard animals that poisoned you when you licked the paint off, or one pair of roller skates between two of us.

All of us, that is to say, except Albert Skinner, who calmly announced that he was asking Father Christmas for the Queen Mary.

None of us said much at the time, but privately we thought Albert was a bit of an optimist. For one thing, the Queen Mary was so big and so grand and so lit-up that it was probably not even for sale. For another, we were all well aware that Father Christmas's representative in the Skinner household was a sullen, foul-tempered collier who also happened to be unemployed.

Albert's birthday present, it was generally known, had been a pair of boots.

Even so, Albert continued to insist that he was getting the Queen Mary for Christmas, and sometimes when we went to his house to swop comics he would look to his father for confirmation.

'Dad, I am, aren't I? Aren't I, dad! Getting that Queen Mary for Christmas?'

Mr Skinner, dourly whittling a piece of wood by the fireside after the habit of all the local miners, would growl without looking up:

'You'll get a clout over the bloody earhole if you don't stop nattering.'

Albert would turn complacently to us. 'I am, see. I'm getting the Queen Mary.'

Sometimes, when his father was in a bad mood (which was quite often), Albert's pleas for reassurance would meet with a more vicious response. 'Will you shut up about the bloody Queen Mary!' Mr Skinner would shout. 'You gormless little get, do you think I'm made of money?'

Outside, his ear tingling from the blow his father had landed on it, Albert would bite back the tears and declare stubbornly: 'I'm still getting it. You wait till Christmas.'

One day the crippled lad at No. 43 was taken by the Church Ladies' Guild to see the military striking clock in the City Arcade, and when he came home he reported that the model of the Queen Mary was no longer in the window of the fabulous toyshop.

'I know,' said Albert. 'I'm getting it for Christmas.'

Then it was Christmas morning, and we all flocked out into the street to show off our presents, sucking our brand-new torches to make our cheeks glow red, or brandishing a lead soldier or two in the pretence that we had a whole regiment of them indoors.

No one expected to see Albert, but before long he came leaping, jumping, almost somersaulting, into the street. 'I've got it! I've got it!'

We clustered round him, and bubbling with pride he produced what seemed on first inspection to be a length of wood. Then we saw that it had been carved at both ends to make a bow and a stern, and that three cotton-reels had been nailed to it for funnels. A row of tin-tacks marked the Plimsoll line, and there were stuck-on bits of cardboard for the portholes. The whole thing was painted over in sticky lamp-black, except for the lettering on the port-side.

'ThE QuEEn MaRy,' it said in white.

Once again, we didn't say much. Albert's Queen Mary was a

73

crude piece of work, but clearly many hours of labour, and much love, had gone into it. Its clumsy contours alone must have taken night upon night of whittling by the fireside.

Mr Skinner, pyjama-jacket tucked into his trousers, had come out of the house and was standing by his garden-gate. Albert, in a rush of happiness, ran to his father and flung his arms around him and hugged him.

'Look, dad! Look what I've got for Christmas!'

'Get out of it, you soft little bugger' said Mr Skinner. He drew contentedly on his empty pipe, cuffed Albert over the head as a matter of habit, and went indoors.

Getting The Pip

The most horrible innovation in the last few years is the new-fangled Greenwich time signal, apparently introduced because the world's clock watcher can no longer be relied upon to count up to six.

You will know that instead of the familiar half dozen pips we now get five pips and a peep.

The Greenwich peep has the effect of fingernails scraping down a window pane. It is a wrong note on an out-of-tune tin whistle. It is the dentist's drill exploring an upper molar. It is the oscillation from Daventry and Hilversum on an old-fashioned wireless. It is Tugboat Annie going down for the third time. It is the fork missing its target in the pickle jar.

Fewer peeps and more pips would be all right by me.

Talking Of Dogs

Excuse me, Waterhouse. I didn't want to bother you during the coal crisis, but now that things have quietened down a bit I have a bone to pick.

Oh, yes? Who is that speaking?

Me. Here. Behind you. The dog.

The dog? You must be out of your tiny canine mind! Don't you realise that I am in the middle of some very important work? I have neither the time nor the inclination to bandy words with a pea-brained Norwich terrier.

That's the bone I wanted to pick with you, Waterhouse. You don't write nearly enough about dogs. It's beginning to get you talked about.

Are you sure you've come to the right column? This is supposed to be a serious political forum, not a bloody pet-shop.

That's what you think. Nobody wants to read all that tripe and rubbish about Harold Wilson, whoever he may be. They want to read about dogs. Tell them about that trick of mine – where I roll over and die for my country.

I shall do no such thing. It's a stupid trick, anyway. If you knew how silly you looked you'd stop doing it.

How about my appealing little ways, then? Tell them how I put my head on one side when I want to go walkies.

When you want to go WHAT?

Walkies.

Now look here, dog, I'm prepared to put up with a great deal but I will not have those twee, nauseating, revolting expressions in my column. Go away and dig up a bone or something.

Not until you've written something about dogs.

I have nothing to say about dogs.

I bet you'd find something to say about dogs if I were to bite you in the leg, wouldn't you? Anyway you could tell them about that black Labrador.

Which black Labrador?

The one you saw with that chap.

What chap?

The business gent on the number 27 bus. And he was talking to this black Labrador.

So he was talking to his dog. There's nothing so very unusual about that.

Tell them the whole story, Waterhouse.

How the hell can I, dog? They wouldn't believe me.

They would if I bit them all in the leg.

Well, it's not really a story. It's just that this chap was sitting on the front seat of a number 27 with his briefcase, his Evening Standard and his black Labrador, and he was reading bits out of the paper.

Aloud?

Yes.

75

To the dog?

Yes.

Well go on, then.

There's nothing else to say. He was just sitting there saying things like: 'What a shame, they want to pull down all those lovely Chinese restaurants in Gerrard Street and build a telephone exchange.' And the dog was just sitting on the floor, looking up at him and listening. That's all.

And you claim you've nothing to say about dogs?

I haven't. If you ask me anything, they were both pie-eyed.

Anyway, you promised to write a column about it.

I said nothing of the sort. I said if I got a quiet day I'd try to find room for a paragraph.

If I refrain from biting you in the leg, will you write a column about it?

The Button Fair

On Easter Saturday the proper fair opened for business on the flat patch of cinders that called itself the town moor. By Easter Sunday we were all broke. On Easter Monday the Button Fair began.

When I mentioned the Button Fair in passing some months ago, I was delighted to hear from many readers that it still goes on, although it has been hit by inflation like everything else.

A fourer is now a niner and a fiver is now a twelver. At least it shows that decimalisation has not caught up with the Button Fair. And as for those hexagonal pearl buttons . . .

But before going into the hexagonal pearl button question I had better clue-in those readers unfortunate enough not to have been raised in the city of Leeds, which is where it all happens.

You go to the Easter fair clutching your life-savings and you squander the lot on the roll-'em-down stall and the coconut shy. This takes about one and a half minutes. Spending your bus fare on a last wild fling at hoop-la takes another two seconds.

With the smell of roast chestnuts, diesel oil, over-heated generators and toffee apples still singeing your nostrils, you trudge home and try to perpetuate that brief enjoyment.

A chalked grid on the pavement becomes the roll-'em-down

stall. A Webley airgun and a milk bottle have the makings of a rifle range. A pedal-car with three wheels stands in for the dodgems.

And the currency is buttons. All kinds of buttons, including embossed army buttons which are as rare and precious as pieces of eight, but excluding shirt buttons, which have the spurious value of those little Arab coins with holes in the middle.

In that pre-inflationary era when I had the hoop-la concession – you can make a good hoop-la stall if you know where to lay your hands on a set of pram tyres – a trouser button counted as one.

One what? The question was never asked. Whenever the Button Fair took place it was universally recognised that a trouser button was the lowest coin of the realm of children's play. It was a one-er, everyone knew it was a one-er, and that was that.

A jacket button was a twoer. An overcoat button was a three-er. A cloth-covered button – snipped, as likely as not, from your sister's best coat – was a fourer. A pearl button, such as a mother might find mysteriously missing from the baby's matinée jacket, was a sixer.

And a hexagonal pearl button ... but we will come to hexagonal pearl buttons in a moment.

With your pockets weighed down with purloined buttons, you were a rich man indeed when you strolled through the sideshows of the Button Fair. You could risk a trouser button on the coconut shy (which was probably rigged) pay out a twoer for a ride on a scooter to the end of the street and back lose a sixer on the turn of a card at the Find the Lady stall, run by the button equivalent of Soho sharks.

But the curious thing about the Button Fair was that for all its liveliness it was only a peripheral aspect of our mania for buttons. The real interest, while the craze lasted, was in the miniature reproduction of the capitalist system that we created, down to the last detail.

We had button banks and a button exchange; button speculators who cornered the trouser button market and sold at a profit; button lenders who charged a criminal rate of interest; button brokers who would float the capital needed to set up a stall and rake in their commission.

We even had a crooked button financier, a nine-year-old

wheeler-dealer whose immense button fortune was believed stolen from Montague Burton's. It was this Bent Button King who was responsible for the spectacular crash of the hexagonal pearl button.

The hexagonal pearl button was, by virtue of its great rarity, size, beauty and unusual shape, a twenty-fiver. Many of us knew it only by reputation there were rumoured to be only six pearl hexagonals in existence, floated into the currency from an evening gown bought at a jumble sale.

Then one day the Bent Button King flooded the market with a shoeboxful of pearl hexagonals, acquired from the same doubtful source as all his previous wealth.

The effect on the button exchange was sensational. Within minutes the pearl hexagonal had been devalued from a twenty-fiver to a niner. Pearl matinée jacket ordinaries correspondingly plunged from six to four; the blazer button dived down to a twoer; the humble trouser button was worthless. Button fortunes were wiped out overnight. Button brokers shut up shop and went back to playing cowboys and Indians.

That was the last Button Fair I can remember. I am glad to hear that the currency has since been restored and the trouser button is now a twoer.

It was a good feeling to be rich in buttons. Their only use, of course, was to acquire more buttons, but that after all is the true purpose of capital. None of us had twopence in real money to rub together, but while the Button Fair lasted we lived like millionaires.

The Concrete Midas

Someone, somehow, some day, has got to halt the terrifying march of the property developers.

They are like locusts. Homes, pubs, shops, department stores, theatres, avenues of trees, village streets, Georgian squares, well-loved landmarks, all crumble into dust at their approach.

They would tear down St Paul's Cathedral itself if they had the chance.

They leave desolation in their wake. Mournful lawns and rain-swept piazzas. Clusters of office towers like gigantic liquorice allsorts. Drizzling fountains. Subterranean shopping precincts where the footsteps echo.

The wind howls along the cat-walks and the daffodils wilt in the concrete tubs. Felt-tipped obscenities appear on the mosaic walls of the pedestrian tunnels. Nowhere to go and nothing to do. A brand-new slum is born.

In London alone the developers must have pulled down more famous buildings than were ever destroyed in the blitz. Elsewhere, towns that never heard the wail of a siren are beginning to look like the victims of a thousand-bomber raid.

All so that a handful of companies may pay through the nose for executive offices the size of bingo halls. And so that the property barons may grow even more disgustingly rich than they are already.

There was a time when self-made tycoons performed some public service to earn their millions. They sold tea or made soap or invented the pneumatic bicycle tyre or opened a great shopping emporium. They stimulated trade. They created employment. They endowed art galleries and put up statues and built model villages. They were ebullient men who added to the zest of life.

Build a better mouse-trap, they used to say in those days, and the world will beat a path to your door. Today the secret of success is to build a bigger rat-trap.

The quickest way and practically the only way to make a million in this age of opportunity is to buy a street where people live, work, shop and play, and strangle it. Destroy their homes, scatter their friendships, obliterate their favourite walks, sell off their memories to the junkyard or the antique supermarket.

And build. Upwards. Another prestige office block from the Midas who turns everything he touches into concrete.

Why property developers are so called is a mystery, for when they swoop on some unsuspecting neighbourhood they do not develop it, they stultify it.

They halt, at a stroke, the constant, subtle and apparently haphazard process of regeneration by which our cities have stayed alive for centuries. They institute a process of asphyxiation by blueprint known as 'comprehensive development'. When the scaffolding comes down and the bulldozers have moved on, a once-bustling centre has been petrified so successfully that it might as well be covered in volcanic lava, like Pompeii.

The authors of this devastation may line their own pockets but they do not add to the wealth of the nation by as much as threepence. They do not create trade. They do not encourage commerce. They produce nothing. And yet, like Viking plunderers, they seem to have a free run of the land to take all they want and destroy what they please.

There will come a time when we look around this country for the places we once loved, the unexpected corners, the hidden little squares, the buildings that were never ancient monuments but were sturdy, useful and pleasing to the eye, the streets that turned and twisted for no good reason, the alleys, the cul-de-sacs and crescents, and town parks the size of pocket handkerchiefs.

And we will find them all gone. All of them.

It will be too late then to shout in anger down the concrete canyons.

Death Of A Salesman

The trouble with door-to-door salesmanship is that it provides a classic example of the irresistible force meeting the immovable housewife.

The salesman wants to sell a vacuum-cleaner and the housewife has no intention of buying one. There is therefore a conflict of interests which has got to be settled somehow.

If the foot-in-the-door man knows his job the deadlock will be settled in his favour. He will unload not only a vacuum-cleaner but also twenty-five optional extras including a cake-crumb brush, an anti-spider's web nozzle, a tin-tack detector and a special device for sweeping out the dog kennel.

Not to my surprise, some MPs have been speaking up against the technique of the hard sell. What is slightly puzzling is how they hope to put a stop to it. It is a highly tenacious profession they are tangling with. They might just as well legislate to stop club bores from telling long jokes.

There is only one way to emerge unscathed from an encounter with a seasoned high-pressure salesman and that is to be as tough and thick-skinned as he is. Allow me – this won't take a minute, lady, don't shut the door – to give you the benefit of my own experience.

Many years ago it came to me in a vision that what I needed to make life complete was an expensive, multi-volume encyclopedia. From Aabenraa to Zygadenus this storehouse of knowledge stretched along four feet of bookshelf, it cost the equivalent of six weeks' pay, and I meant to have it.

A few days after I had reached this monumental decision the doorbell rang and there on the welcome mat was a young man who, by his briefcase, his fixed smile and his polished shoes – one of them with a slight dent in it – could only be an encyclopedia salesman. A happy coincidence.

'Good morning, sir. As a family man, you must be deeply concerned with your children's education . . .'

'Say no more,' I said. 'You have a customer.'

The happy smile faded. The eyes narrowed. The doorstep whizzkid assumed the cautious expression of a doorstep whizzkid who is being taken for a ride.

'Come in,' I said, 'and I'll give you a cheque.'

He followed me reluctantly into the living-room and perched unhappily on the edge of the sofa. He dived into his briefcase and fished out a handful of brochures. These seemed to restore his confidence.

'Now sir, I won't insult your intelligence by pretending that this de-luxe set of encyclopedias in its own finely-finished mahogany case is inexpensive. But when you consider the many hours of education and instruction which you can enjoy for less than the price of a packet of cigarettes per day . . .'

'You never spoke a truer word,' I said, cheque-book poised. 'What's the date?'

Whizzkid tugged nervously at his collar. Whatever he'd learned about selling encyclopedias on his training course, clearly they hadn't told him how to deal with someone who actually wanted to buy the damn things.

'Of course,' he gabbled on, continuing the spiel, 'there is no need for you to pay a lump sum. We have an easy payments plan which, over two years . . .'

'No thanks,' I said. 'I'll pay cash on the nail.'

He still thought there was a catch in it somewhere.

'You do realise how much the de-luxe set costs?'

'Sure,' I said. 'Cheap at the price.'

'We do have an economically-priced edition printed on thin paper in five volumes. Would you like me to show you a leaflet?'

'No thanks. I want the full works. The entire leather-bound de-luxe production.'

'You wouldn't prefer to think it over?' he asked hopefully.

'I've thought it over,' I snapped back, getting testy. 'Now are you going to sell me your wretched encyclopedia or not?'

The reluctant salesman made one last desperate throw for my non-custom.

'You're sure you really need this expensive work?'

'Of course I really need it! I wouldn't be buying it if I didn't!'

'What I mean is, if you use an encyclopedia only on rare occasions, you might find it more practical to go down to the public library.'

'Look,' I said. 'I've made a cheque out. I want your encyclopedia. All four foot of it. Do I get it or not?'

I fixed him with a steady gaze. His eyes dropped guiltily, and he closed his briefcase.

'I'll leave you a brochure and some forms to fill in,' he mumbled. 'Then if you haven't changed your mind in, say, a week's time, we can get it all finalised.'

He slunk out, a broken, bewildered man, and I never saw him again.

As I said, you've got to be tough with these super-salesmen.

Take My Word

I see that a lady called Miss Olive Behan has been declared National Scrabble Champion. There has, of course, been a ridiculous mistake.

Miss Behan is not the National Scrabble Champion. I am.

It is technically true that I did not bother to enter the contest where this strange championship was decided. That was only because I thought my own claim was beyond dispute.

I must be the only man in the world – bar of course my opponent – who has played Scrabble non-stop for three and a half months, pausing only for sleep and food.

My grasp of the Scrabble vocabulary is unsurpassed. Xi: the fourteenth letter of the Greek alphabet. Xyst: a covered portico. Xeric: of, pertaining to, or adapted to a dry environment. Xat: a carved totem pole.

Now I will tell you how these valuable words came into my possession.

Some years ago my friend Willis Hall and I, at great expense, hired an office high up in the rafters of Shaftesbury Avenue with the object of writing a play.

In order to write a play you have to have an idea for a play, and this ingredient was momentarily lacking. What we did possess, however, was a Scrabble board, left behind by a previous tenant.

It seemed a good way of getting through an unproductive morning. Educational, too. There is nothing like Scrabble for improving your word-power.

Za: the seventeenth letter of the Arabic alphabet. Zakah: a poor-relief tax once imposed in the Yemen. Zax: a tool for punching holes in slate.

When you are working on a play and the paper is still blank after twenty-one days it is easy to persuade yourself that you are waiting for inspiration. When you have been placing small plastic tiles on a numbered grid for the same length of time it is easy to fool yourself that you can take Scrabble or leave it alone.

Wrong. We were hooked. Addicted. We tried to kick the habit a couple of times but there are serious withdrawal symptoms. You stare at the typewriter and the keys seem to re-arrange themselves into obscure words.

Ixtle: the fibre of certain tropical plants. Zonda: a hot, oppressive wind in the Argentine pampas. Zowie: an expression of keen pleasure used by Scrabble-players who have just made a triple-letter score.

I see that Miss Olive Behan caused a stir at the National Scrabble jousts by coming up with the archaic word Quean, meaning a loose-living woman. Childsplay. I would like to ask the Pretender to the Scrabble Crown what she would do with this unpromising collection of letters: XPYDIIU.

What you do is shuffle them round a bit, hitch them to the back end of the word Em (a printer's measure) and make Pyxidium, a seed vessel which dehisces transversely. And not only does it dehisce transversely, it also gives you a fantastic score, for you get a hefty points bonus for using all your letters in one go.

I will come clean and admit that I never got Pyxidium but one midnight when we were twelve weeks into the game I was within an ace of reaching it. Another month and I might have made it.

But when the rent bills turned to red and the children began to whine for vitamins, Mr Hall and I proved ourselves to be men of iron will. Recognising that there is no known cure for Scrabble-mania except total abstinence, we threw the whole bag of tricks down the lift-shaft, put a sheet of paper in the typewriter, and wrote the words 'Act One, Scene One'.

We went home and had a refreshing night's sleep and next morning, bright and early, Mr Hall turned up for duty with a Monopoly set under his arm.

As well as being the National Scrabble Champion, I am also the National Monopoly Champion.

How Long, O Lord . . . ?

And God said unto Noah, Make thee an ark of gopher wood; rooms shalt thou make in the ark, and the length of the ark shall be 300 cubits.

And of every living thing of all flesh, two of every sort shalt thou bring into the ark, to keep them alive with thee.

And Noah said, Sign here, and leavest Thou a deposit.

And the Lord signed there, and left He a deposit.

And Noah was 600 years old when the flood of waters was upon the Earth.

And the Lord said unto Noah, Where is the ark, which I commanded thee to build?

And Noah said unto the Lord, Verily, I have had three carpenters off ill.

The gopher wood supplier hath let me down – yea, even though the gopher wood hath been on order for nigh upon 12 months. The damp-course specialist hath not turned up. What can I do, O Lord?

And God said unto Noah, I want that ark finished even after seven days and seven nights.

And Noah said, It will be so.

And it was not so.

And the Lord said unto Noah, What seemeth to be the trouble this time?

And Noah said unto the Lord, Mine sub-contractor hath gone bankrupt. The pitch which Thou commandest me to put on the outside and on the inside of the ark hath not arrived. The plumber hath gone on strike.

Noah rent his garments and said, The glazier departeth on holiday to Majorca – yea, even though I offerest him double time. Shem, my son, who helpeth me on the ark side of the business, hath formed a pop group with his brothers Ham and Japheth. Lord, I am undone.

And God said in his wrath, Noah, do not thou mucketh Me about.

The end of all flesh is come before me; for the Earth is filled with violence through them; and behold, I will destroy them with the Earth. How can I destroy them with the Earth if thou art incapable of completing the job that thou was contracted to do?

And Noah said, Lo, the contract will be fulfilled.

And Lo, it was not fulfilled.

And Noah said unto the Lord, The gopher wood is definitely in the warehouse. Verily, and the gopher wood supplier waiteth only upon his servant to find the invoices before he delivereth the gopher wood unto me.

And the Lord grew angry and said, Scrubbeth thou round the gopher wood. What about the animals?

Of fowls after their kind, and of cattle after their kind, of every creeping thing of the Earth after his kind, two of every sort have I ordered to come unto thee, to keep them alive.

Where for example, are the giraffes?

And Noah said unto the Lord, They are expected today.

And the Lord said unto Noah, And where are the clean beasts, the male and the female; to keep their seed alive upon the face of all the Earth?

And Noah said, The van cometh on Tuesday; yea and yea, it will be so.

And the Lord said unto Noah, How about the unicorns?

And Noah wrung his hands and wept, saying, Lord, Lord, they are a discontinued line. Thou canst not get unicorns for love nor money.

And God said, Come thou, Noah, I have left with thee a deposit, and thou hast signed a contract.

Where are the monkeys, and the bears, and the hippopotami, and the elephants, and the zebras and the hartebeests, two of each kind; and of fowls also of the air by sevens, the male and the female?

And Noah said unto the Lord, They have been delivered unto the wrong address, but should arriveth on Friday; all save the fowls of the air by sevens, for it hath just been told unto me that fowls of the air are sold only in half-dozens.

And God said unto Noah, Thou hast not made an ark of gopher wood, nor hast thou lined it with pitch within and without; and of every living thing of all flesh, two of every sort hast thou failed to bring into the ark. What sayest thou, Noah?

And Noah kissed the Earth and said, Lord, Lord, thou knowest in thy wisdom what it is like with delivery dates.

And the Lord in his wisdom said, Noah, my son, I knowest. Why else dost thou think I have caused a flood to descend upon the Earth?

Juke-box Jurist

Police Five. Landlords of several pubs in Central London are worried about the activities of a vandal who is apparently seized by a maniacal hatred of juke-boxes.

His method is simple but diabolical. It is to select the loudest record on the juke-box, feed the machine with coins so that it plays the same tune over and over and over again, and then drift away.

One landlord complains that after the vandal visited his premises, the juke-box seemed to go berserk and refused to play anything except 'Amazing Grace' for the rest of the evening.

Another licensee reports that three men came into his pub at opening time, and that although they must have known the place had been converted a great expense into a doubles bar, they affected a display of surprise at the shiny new juke-box.

One of them was heard to remark: 'I thought this was still a public house. As I perceive it is now a bloody discotheque, I suggest we take our custom elsewhere.'

Before leaving, however, this gang of anti-social elements held a huddled conference where the ringleader appeared to take up a silver collection. He was seen to pour all this money into the juke-box and was subsequently observed pressing buttons.

The juke-box then commenced to play Gilbert O'Sullivan's 'Ooh wakka doo wakka day' thirty-six times in succession.

Some landlords, particularly in the Fleet Street area, believe they know the identity of the vandal. He is said to be a newspaper columnist who believes that a pub should be a place where you are able to talk, drink, play darts and occasionally sing to the accompaniment of a tinny piano.

What a pub should not be, according to this madman's theories, is a place where you are deafened by gramophone records from morning till night.

Mr K. Waterhouse, described as a newspaper columnist, was questioned about his part in the affair last night. Giving his name as Christopher Ward of the *Daily Sketch*, he stated: 'I do not know what you are talking about. I would sooner swim five lengths in the main sewer than cross the threshold of any pub that boasted a juke-box.

'If I happen to wander into one of my regular pubs and find that it has turned itself into a licensed echo-chamber for one of these infernal fairground Daleks, I make a point of never going there again. By the way, can you possibly give me change of a pound in fivepenny pieces?'

This statement is regarded as ambiguous and a close watch is being kept on the columnist's movements. It is thought in informed circles, however, that the true identity of the self-appointed juke-box vigilante will remain for ever shrouded in mystery, like that of Jack the Ripper.

Like, Be Prepared

There is no one quite so dated as the man who tries desperately to keep up to date. It is depressing to see that the Scout Movement of America has made an ass of itself by rewriting its handbook in what it imagines to be the language of the Seventies.

Groovily clicking its fingers – as a substitute for rubbing two sticks together? – it welcomes tenderfoots to the camp fire with a cry of: 'Man, scouting is a ball!' Its recipe for pancakes is to follow the instructions on the packet. Its advice on how to deal with a nosebleed is: 'Keep your cool.' General hints for a good Scout: 'Don't be a wise guy or a loudmouth.'

I am glad to see that there is none of this nonsense in the latest edition of Baden-Powell's chummy classic, 'Scouting for Boys'. Although it has been revised to the extent of taking some dated stuff out, it still retains that old magic flavour of woodsmoke, burned sausages and damp tarpaulin.

The chaps are still addressed as 'fellows' and B-P still regales them with his yarns about Kaffirs, Ghurkas and the Matabele, the moral of which is to keep your eyes open and your bowels active.

My favourite chapter – the one beginning: 'It may happen to some of you that one day you will be the first to find the body of a dead man' – is still intact, and so is the robust advice about smoking, drinking, and other secret vices:

'Just make up your mind for yourself that you don't mean to smoke till you are grown up, and stick to it. That will show you how to be a man much more than any slobbering about with a half-smoked cigarette between your lips.'

Good, hectoring stuff – as similar to the pre-war *Chums Annual* as its updated American equivalent is to *Oz* or *Rolling Stone*. Guess which will survive the longest.

Days Of My Youth

When decimalisation had to do with sums at school, and cabbage white butterflies were as common as wasps, Bank Holiday Monday fell at the beginning instead of at the end of August.

The street was quiet then, for everybody who was anybody took care to be away at the fashionable resorts of Scarborough, Bridlington or Cleethorpes.

The families remaining – ourselves, the Skinners, the Bullocks, and a mighty dynasty called the Cooligans whose tribe had increased so prodigiously that they had been allocated two council houses knocked into one – did not like to admit that they couldn't afford to go on holiday.

So, as they fed the neighbours' cats or attended to the budgies that had been left in their care, our mothers said to each other: 'We thought we'd just go away by the day this year.'

It made sense, they all agreed. Why fritter your money away on boarding-houses when you could spend it on travel? See the world and sleep in your own bed — what happier compromise could any reasonable child hope for?

The Skinner kids and the Bullock kids and I were suitably impressed, and a thrill of pleasure shuddered through the infinite battalions of Cooligans, already gathering hopefully on their twin doorsteps.

Trips to the moors! Streamlined coaches with adjustable seats, gliding past the sweating cyclists on the hills of Whitby! Pea and pie suppers on Lake Windermere! Late-night excursion trains steaming back from Morecambe! And tomorrow . . . well, we'd stick another pin in the map and see where fortune took us.

We began to feel sorry for our conventional friends on their orthodox holidays, toiling day after day up the lighthouse steps at Flamborough Head, or waking up in their caravans and seeing the same yawning expanse of golden sand.

We, the last of the merchant adventurers, were going away by the day this year. It was a solemn promise.

On Bank Holiday Monday, it turned out, we did not go away for the day. Apparently this was standard practice. The trains were too full and the tram schedules were erratic, and there was not enough bread to make sandwiches. Anyone with any experience of going away by the day knew it was bad thinking to start such a programme on Bank Holiday Monday.

On Tuesday we had a communal picnic in the local park — ourselves, the Skinners and the Bullocks. What we were doing, the mothers told each other, was gradually breaking ourselves in, casting our sights on ever-widening horizons as the week wore on. Today the municipal boating lake — tomorrow the world.

The Cooligans did not go to the park. The Cooligans did not go anywhere, ever. There were in fact whole squadrons of Cooligans who had never been further than the end of the street in their lives. But it was polite to accept the fiction that they too were going away by the day this year.

Wednesday was a rest day. We children, it was thought, were prone to over-excitement, nervous exhaustion, sunburn and travel sickness. It would do us no harm to play quietly in the street with the unfortunate Cooligans.

On Thursday there were a few spots of rain before breakfast. This made travelling a risky business. Our mothers discussed the treacherous weather: the possibility of snow on the moors, blinding sleet on the far side of the Pennines, and the sheet of fog that most likely hung like a tarpaulin over the entire east coast.

We frolicked in the boiling sun with the wretched Cooligans, taking care not to taunt them with the news of tomorrow's outing to Belle Vue zoo in Manchester.

But Friday, dawning in a silver haze, brought a minor setback to our plans. The excitements of the week had taken their toll: the Skinners had upset stomachs and the rest of us were suspected of sickening for colds. Better be sensible and leave the zoo for another day.

On Saturday, of course, we couldn't go anywhere, for that was the day the neighbours came back from the seaside. Clutching their cardboard suitcases and brandishing their giant mint humbugs they trooped down the street boasting and bragging about clean sheets and egg-and-bacon breakfasts, jugs of tea on the sands, pier concerts, mystery tours and hour after hour of unbroken sunshine.

And at last they asked us what kind of week we'd had of it.

'Oh, very nice, thank you for enquiring. We just went away by the day this year.'

The Cooligans, streaming out of their double-fronted council barracks until the street was packed with them as far as the eye could see, naturally had to go and put the cherry on the icing.

'We had a lovely time, didn't we, Mrs Skinner? Going to different places every day. Lake Windermere, Blackpool, More-cambe, Whitby – we went all over.'

Our mothers smiled tolerantly at the deception, but none of us gave the Cooligans away. Why should we, when we'd had such a grand holiday – just going away by the day?

The Cheese And I

Let us sing in praise of cheese – making sure that we get the tune right.

We will hit a wrong note if we sing of cheese with holes in it, cheese with the consistency of lard, or that which looks, tastes and smells like a wayside shelter for homeless maggots.

Those are foreign cheeses. Foreign cheeses have their own song and they may sing it themselves – while on the march.

Our anthem is for English cheese. It is for crumbly Cheshire and blue-veined Stilton, for Double Gloucester, Leicester, Derby Sage and Wensleydale. Especially Wensleydale.

Wensleydale has the colour and texture of a milkmaid's shoulder and when you bite into it you have a sensation of being tickled at the back of the throat by buttercups.

The English Country Cheese Council – a professional choir to augment our amateur glee-club – have launched a campaign to promote English cheese. I hope they sell it by the cartload. In particular I hope that a wedge or two will tip the scales of the curmudgeonly cheesemonger who educated me to Wensleydale.

We have sung of English cheese; let us now sing of Family Purvis Grocer, Supplier of Quality Provisions Since 1872.

I'd spent a few days in a small Yorkshire market town and I wanted to take home a trifling souvenir. I'd noticed, in the tiny supermarket, some attractive stone jars, decorated with a pastoral scene, and containing cheese. Ideal.

But opposite the supermarket was a ramshackle shop with its name emblazoned in gold letters – *Family* in an elaborate italic scroll, PURVIS in bold, many-seriffed capitals, and *Grocer* in italics again, completing the pleasing typographical symmetry.

Although it was market day, the shop was deserted. The saw-dust floor might not have seen a human footprint since the first Purvis began supplying quality provisions a century ago. I decided to give this neglected business my custom.

I stepped into a miniature emporium that could have been a corner of Harrods' food hall during a power cut. The sunlight was obscured by a row of great swinging hams with cloves stuck in them like mapping pins. Huge cartwheel cheeses cast a brooding shade over pyramids of butter. Platoons of fat poultry nestled cool and safe on the north side of a mountain of brown eggs.

Flitting about behind all this produce was a blurred stooping figure in a white apron. Family Purvis Grocer himself.

'I would like,' I said, since he showed no disposition to open the conversation, 'one of those little stone jars of cheese.'

Nothing happened for a full minute. Then a malevolent, grizzled face peered out through the gap between two sides of bacon.

'I won't have them on the premises!' snarled Family Purvis Grocer, and disappeared.

Talking into thin air, I remarked that that was a pity as I'd hoped to take one back to London as a present. A derisive laugh rang out from the shadows.

'You'll be better off with a tin of Harrogate toffee!'

A weevil apprehended in Family Purvis Grocer's sugar could not have felt more uncomfortable than I was feeling now. Toying unhappily with a presentation barrel of biscuits, I became aware of a beady eye fixed on me from its hidey-hole between the sides of bacon.

'If you want to take something back,' said Family Purvis Grocer grudgingly, 'you'd better have a bit of Wensleydale.'

What? As a present? A lump of cheese wrapped in greaseproof paper?

'They'll thank you for it. How much do you want?'

About to slink out of the shop, I blundered against one of the swinging hams. I must have panicked, for I heard myself babbling that I'd take half a pound. And a look of satanic glee flashed across Family Purvis Grocer's lugubrious features.

'What month?'

Month? What was he rambling on about now?

'Cheese,' explained Family Purvis Grocer, speaking slowly as if to a simpleton, 'has to mature. You don't want it too young and you don't want it too old. So what month do you want?'

'February,' I said wildly.

'You want April,' he said, and sliced a wire through one of the pristine cartwheels with the skill and devotion of a sculptor carving marble. A creamy wedge was placed before me and Family Purvis Grocer folded his arms – sardonically.

'Aren't you going to wrap it?' I asked at length.

A withering stare. 'You're supposed to *taste* cheese!'

So I tasted it. The tickle of buttercups at the back of the throat. Delicious.

Family Purvis Grocer's last words as I shambled out into the sunlight were: 'And tell them not to put it in the fridge!'

But I didn't. I didn't tell them anything. I took my half pound of Wensleydale back to the hotel and scoffed it myself – every blessed crumb. And took home a tin of Harrogate toffee.

Blackberry Fair

This year, among other delights, I have sat in St Mark's Square in Venice and tramped across Wharfedale. I have re-read some favourite books when the rain was beating against the window and I have eaten a few good dinners with old friends.

But if you were to ask me what I have enjoyed the most, I would have to reply that it was the locating, picking and eventual consumption (in the shape of a pie) of two and three quarter pounds of blackberries.

This was not only on a Sabbath morning but in a Royal park to boot. So as well as breaking Henry VIII's Sunday observance laws I was probably also guilty of filching the Queen's fruit. In the rosy glow of these balmy autumn days, however, I feel sure of a pardon from the monarch. For my part, though a life-long Republican, I will readily concede that she can keep her swans if I can have her blackberries.

Blackberrying – or blackbegging as we used to call it in those far-off days when every hedgerow seemed like an adjunct of the Golliberry factory – is at the same time the simplest and most subtle of all outdoor activities.

It combines the utter peace of a ramble through the woods with the excitement of a steeplechase. It encourages companionship and yet promotes bitter rivalry. It proves the paradoxical truth that while real joy springs from unselfishness it also springs – as any Paul Getty of the jam-jars full well knows – from sheer acquisitiveness.

Every seasoned blackberry-picker sets off on the principle that it is better to travel unhopefully than to arrive. The mood is one of complacent pessimism. If the brambles have not been picked clean by birds then they must either have fallen prey to some weird environmental blight or been ravaged by picnickers.

What you are doing, you tell yourself, is merely taking the kids for a walk – and you happen to have these jam-jars.

With any luck, you soon establish that to have arrived in some uncharted fruity Valhalla is infinitely more satisfying than to have travelled in whatever frame of mind.

From a thicket half-swathed in mist you hear an excited tally-ho: 'Here's some!' And far away in the middle of the woods, where you had half-feared that a good proportion of your children must have fallen into a bog or been seized by rapists, you hear a faint answering cry: 'There's some here too, and they're GI-NORMOUS!'

You stumble through the undergrowth in the direction of the best offer and suddenly a shaft of sunlight, like the rainbow falling on the crock of gold, illuminates about an acre of black-berries. They shimmer, all plump and purple in the sun, like a purée of rubies or sapphires, and they are not only GI-NORMOUS, they are the size of crab-apples.

You call across the crisp autumn air: 'Just a minute – got a stone in my shoe.' And craftily, furtively, like Midas given a ten-minute reprieve, you proceed to stuff your jam-jar with luscious berries.

Meanwhile the cries of triumph have mysteriously ceased. You catch an occasional glimpse of your children flitting silently from one bush to another, their jam-jars jealously hidden under coat or sweater. They wave feebly, trying to look as if they are chasing late butterflies.

Serendipity – the almost lost art of making happy discoveries by accident – is what blackberrying is basically all about. More peripherally it involves hands stained the colour of walnuts and good clothes plucked to shreds by brambles; meeting on the woodland path to compare the morning's haul; shrill cries of abuse and shame from those whose jam-jar of booty barely touches the Plimsoll line, and furthermore contains unripe berries; smugness from those who lifted the innermost branches and found the glistening lode-star.

But when your squashy plunder is borne home in triumph and weighed in, like an Ascot winner, all the selfish quibbling is forgotten, and there is a corporate glow of common achievement.

The fruit is ceremonially topped, washed, cooked, and given a crown of flaky pastry. The culmination of the day's scratchy endeavour is a blackberry pie of satisfying proportions.

It looks like all the days of autumn encapsulated under a golden crust; it tastes of ambrosia; and its after-taste, which lingers on into the chilly evening, is of late sunshine, friendship, memories of the lanes of childhood, and all the good things of life.

Tea And Symphony

According to some nonsense in the paper, the computerised day is coming when housewives will no longer have to go out shopping. They'll simply press a few buttons on a console and the stuff will be automatically delivered from the warehouse.

A likely story. If I had a pound for all the fancy innovations that were about to revolutionise our lives but didn't, I'd be riding around in my own hovercraft by now.

In any case, the idea's old hat. Where I come from, we had that kind of service forty years ago.

People did go out to the shops, mainly for social reasons; but it was possible to buy all the necessities of life without ever stirring out of doors. And we did it without pushing buttons.

What we had was a great nomadic tribe of street vendors. My father was one of them. He sold fruit and vegetables from a horse and cart; and whenever he was detained (on business no doubt) at some hostelry on the far side of the city, his horse – although neither computerised nor remote-controlled – could find its own way home.

This arrangement went on until Leeds got its first traffic lights in 1928. (They were, as a matter of interest, the first traffic lights in Britain.) Not having been informed of this system, the horse ambled through the red and was taken into custody. After this traumatic experience, it refused to travel without the pilot on board.

But I digress. Besides my father's vegetable cart there was also the fried-fish man, the pea-and-pie man, the firewood man, the bread man, the pop man who dispensed lemonade on Sunday mornings, the gipsies hawking clothes pegs and lavender, the scissors-grinder, the chair-mender, the flower-lady, the French onion-seller, the Italian ice-cream man and the Indian herbal medicine man.

We even had a muffin man – or, to be more accurate, a pikelet man – who carried his basket on his head and rang a hand bell. The others (except of course the medicine man, whose ethics forbade him to advertise) relied on a symphony of street-cries. When they were out in force on pay night, they must have sounded like the chorus of a Lionel Bart musical.

I have yet to mention the Tea Man, who was not so much a street hawker as a walking Woolworths. Pins and needles, razor blades, bobbins of cotton, press-studs, buttons, boot-laces, tapes and ribbons, hair-slides, shoe polish, zinc ointment, black lead, Donkey stone, soap – he must have carried enough stock to fill three shop counters.

The Tea Man would stand patiently on the doorstep, the heavy tray slung from his shoulders by thick canvas straps, while you browsed over his portable bazaar at leisure. Whatever he didn't have he would fetch the next week, committing effortlessly to memory a hundred tiny orders for combs and collar studs and cards of elastic and gramophone needles.

He was, I suppose, the last of the old-time pedlars, but why he was called the Tea Man was forever a mystery, for the one thing he didn't sell was tea. That was provided on Saturday mornings by the firm of Rington's, who delivered it in a shiny brougham pulled by a smart black horse (though not so smart, I bet, that it could find its own way back to the stable). Perhaps they had an arrangement – Rington's wouldn't sell razor blades if the Tea Man didn't sell tea.

Talking of mysteries, why did the Sunday morning pop man sell slabs of pork dripping on the side? And how did the fried-fish man keep his wares bubbling hot, even in sleet and rain?

But enough of these ramblings. This week, besides the post-man and the newsboy, there was only one itinerant trader in my street. He was the rag-and-bone man, and his mournful if incomprehensible call – 'Hennyrah-boooo!' – reminded me of all the street cries we would be hearing still, if we were not living in better times.

Taking The Credit

The new Access card, whereby all those who can afford to pay cash may now live on credit, is bad news for the makers of trouser-pocket linings. Why weigh yourself down with half-a-pound of loose change when all you need is a ballpoint pen and a plastic ticket?

Like the hot dog, the hamburger, the yo-yo and the Mickey Mouse tee-shirt, this American-inspired wheeze will no doubt catch on. But not, I hope, to the extent to which it has caught on in the Never-never land across the water.

96

In many parts of the United States, folding money is now completely redundant. They will accept your crumpled dollars as a last resort, but not before you've been made to feel that you're spreading germs, encouraging muggers and generally making a nuisance of yourself.

Without a stack of credit cards in your wallet, you are as exposed and embarrassed as if you'd forgotten to put on your underclothes. (American girls, I'm sure, are warned by their mothers to carry a Diners' Club card in case they're run over and have to pay for the ambulance.)

I remember once booking into a Los Angeles hotel where I was handed a form asking me how I proposed to settle my bill. Since I proposed to settle in cash, I wrote 'Cash', and the desk clerk turned white under his California tan. You would have thought I was offering to pay him in Indian beads.

'You don't wish to utilise an accreditisation facility, Mr Waterhouse?' he said in that appalling jargon which I'm sure is now taught in high schools instead of English.

No thank you. I'll pay cash.

'Travellers' cheques, would that be, Mr Waterhouse?'

No. Cash. These things, Dollars.

I showed him a few greenbacks and he stared at them as if they were an interesting collection of foreign stamps.

'One moment, sir.'

He darted into the inner office and I saw secretarial heads craning over the partition and giving me the kind of look I expect they normally reserved for people trying to book in as Mr and Mrs Smith. In a moment the manager appeared.

'Glad to know you, Mr Waterhouse. We hope you'll have a pleasant stay with us, and for your further enjoyment at this time we'd like to extend accreditisation facilities. We accept any regular credit card or if it's your pleasure we'd be happy to bill your company.'

I don't want accreditisation facilities, thank you. I want to pay cash.

Again I produced my wad of dollars pointing out that on each one of them was printed in legible type: 'This note is legal tender for all debts, public and private.'

The manager read the words for himself, checked the signature that had been put to this reckless promise (Dorothy Andrew Katia, Treasurer to the United States), and seemed to waver.

'As a formality, Mr Waterhouse, could I request that you produce some identification at this time?'

I showed him my passport, my driving licence, a bill for the water rates and a letter from my brother. He examined them with care.

'These seem to be in order, Mr Waterhouse. To facilitate our accounting process at this time, could I request that you pay in advance?'

So I coughed up my wretched hoard of dollars and he held them up to the light then put them away in a cupboard. One day, I imagine, he'll take them out and show them to his grandchildren.

I stayed in the hotel a week and every time I entered the foyer a man sitting near the water-cooler lowered his newspaper and gave me a funny look. I learned later that he was the hotel detective. He must have been told to keep an eye on the Limey bum who couldn't afford to live on credit.

Lost, Stolen Or Strayed

This column has had some pretty strange adventures in its time, but never before has it been kidnapped.

The dastardly deed occurred in a train just south of Peterborough. The column was scribbled out on a notepad and I had left it snug as a bug cocooned in a bundle of newspapers.

This column is quite used to being left alone. Give it a bag of crisps and a bottle of lemonade and it will wait outside the saloon bar for hours on end. It knows that it mustn't talk to strangers.

So it was with an easy mind that I tucked it up between the *Daily Telegraph* and the *Financial Times* and went down the corridor for a swift one. The column had been getting overexcited during our journey – it had been carrying on alarming about the American elections – and I thought it could do with a nice quiet snooze. I promised to bring it back a pork pie.

I was in the buffet car for no more than half an hour and when I got back to my empty compartment the column was gone. There was no ransom note and no signs of a struggle. Its bed of newspapers was also missing, so either the column was carried off in its sleep or it was chloroformed to keep it quiet.

When last seen, my column was wearing a fixed grin and it was chuntering on about the willingness of American voters to buy a used hearse from President Nixon. Should anyone sidle up to you in a pub, claiming that a column answering this description has fallen off the back of a lorry, please let me know immediately.

A possibility that cannot be ruled out at this stage is that the kidnapping was organised by a syndicate of international column-snatchers. In that case my column could well have been smuggled out of the country and translated into Hindustani – a linguistic paint-spray job that will make it difficult to trace.

Personally, I do not think we are looking for a gang. I think Interpol, the CID and the FBI would be well advised to watch out for an amateur – a pathetic loner who has always wanted a column of his own and could not resist the temptation of snatching mine. If such an unhappy creature has got my column, I hope he will care for it and not feed it on split infinitives.

There is another wild theory, which I discount completely. That is that after returning from the buffet car after no more than half an hour – certainly no longer than an hour at the very outside – I may have inadvertently wandered into the wrong carriage.

In that case, my faithful column has either been chucked out by British Rail cleaners or it is waiting forlornly for me near the bookstall at King's Cross.

If it should read these lines, it knows that it has only to return home at once and we shall regard the incident as closed.

Put Out More Flags

It's all right as far as it goes to give schoolkids the day off for the Queen's Silver Wedding anniversary. What I want to know, as a connoisseur of these Royal red-letter days, is where is the free milk chocolate?

There was free milk chocolate when King George V celebrated his silver jubilee; free milk chocolate when he came up North to open a clutch of public buildings; free milk chocolate when George VI took over the family business.

99

For those of us with a sweet tooth, it was a great disappointment when Edward VIII ducked out of his coronation. We sang insulting songs about him and Mrs Simpson – not because we were against morganatic marriage as such but because this gravest of all constitutional crises had done us out of our free milk chocolate.

Perhaps I am taking too narrow a view of those historic royal milestones. There are those, I know, who remember the Silver Jubilee not so much for the free milk chocolate as for the tins in which this buckshee confection was contained.

Silver in colour, flat and oblong in shape, and bearing highly-coloured portraits of the monarch and his lady in some incredible Ruritanian get-up, these tins when divested of their contents made useful pencil-boxes – the council's object, I think, in distributing them with such gusto to every school in the city.

Along with the Jubilee tea-caddy, the Jubilee biscuit-barrel, the Jubilee toffee-tin and the Jubilee cake-tin, the Jubilee chocolate-cum-pencil box was given mantelpiece status among the family bric-a-brac.

Eventually the shinier keepsakes of George VI's coronation (most of them in the form of beakers) edged these mementoes of twenty-five glorious years out of fashion. They were relegated to the back of the cupboard and used for storing insurance books or lengths of string. Today you can find them in antique shops.

They are not making these Royal occasions like they used to. Even by today's big-screen standards the Silver Jubilee of 1935 was a smash hit.

The official celebrations were extravagant enough – there were Jubilee banquets, Jubilee concerts, Jubilee stamps, a new Silver Jubilee train that smashed the world speed record; and, of course, free Jubilee chocolate – but even for those times it was extraordinary how the event seized the popular imagination.

In every town and village it was an occasion for bell-ringing and bun-fights. Scouts and guides paraded past every available civic building; patches of waste ground were turned overnight into Jubilee Gardens of Rest; neglected cul-de-sacs were planted with trees and renamed Jubilee Street.

Tree-planting went over big in Jubilee year. In our neighbourhood, as in thousands of others, rows of Silver Jubilee saplings were ceremoniously dug in by local bigwigs. They were promptly uprooted by hooligans and tossed on the Silver Jubilee bonfire.

The centrepiece of the Jubilee junketings, for most of us, was The Street Party. For weeks on end, in preparation for this beano, our mothers had been hoarding lemons, custard powders, currants and raisins, jellies, hundreds and thousands, baking soda, angelica, best butter, lard, cinnamon and all the spices of the Co-op grocery counter.

I have a distinct recollection of being denied cake and buns during the period commencing Jubilee Day Minus Seven: all cake and buns, and the materials for making cake and buns, had been seized by the Housewives' Mafia.

On the morning of Jubilee Day itself, the street took on the appearance of King Arthur's court before an important banquet. A crocodile of kitchen tables, thirty or forty yards long, had been set down the middle of the street and covered with crêpe paper. Serfs and varlets flitted hither and thither arranging chairs, benches, piano-stools, orange-boxes, step-ladders – anything that could be sat on.

Matrons with steaming faces bustled out carrying teacloth-covered trays and jugs of lemonade. Scurvy knaves helped themselves to jam tarts and sausage rolls. Damsels in distress fell into the trifle and had to be taken home to change their party dresses.

Of the actual banquet I remember very little, except that we were given a Union Jack each but had to take our own spoons; and that owing to an administrative error those at the north end of the table had egg sandwiches followed by egg sandwiches, and those at the south end had currant buns followed by currant buns, while I, somewhere in the middle, had an enormous purple jelly all to myself.

At about six o'clock the adult helpers began to sing 'Little Man You've Had A Busy Day' in a pointed manner. The small fry were packed indoors while the banqueting table was cleared for the second sitting – this one for the grown-ups.

They must have been fervent royalists round our way, for very late that night, when I got up to be sick, they were still celebrating the Silver Jubilee. Some were singing, some were dancing, some were just lying there, and a few were clinging to the gate-posts looking very ill indeed. I presumed that like myself they had had too much purple jelly.

Death Of A Clock

I have noticed in my stroll through life that people have much the same relationship with clocks as they have with cats.

It is not the main function of clocks to tell the time, any more than it is the main function of cats to catch mice. Both are there to provide companionship.

They have much else in common. They add colour to the mundane day. They are wilful and eccentric. They amuse. They soothe. They are an endless source of anecdotes.

This is particularly true of alarm clocks. All alarm clocks, however mass produced, are individualists. All alarm clocks are unique.

No alarm clock, however, is as unique as mine, so I shall proceed to tell you about it.

In appearance, it is like a mutant grandfather clock that has been sawn off at the shoulders. It is encased in carved mahogany. It has a stainless steel dial encrusted with brass filigree. Above the dial is a hinged dome, which we will explore in a moment. Below the dial is a little brass tray that looks as if it issues railway platform tickets.

I told you my clock was unique, and you ain't seen nothing yet. Let us lift up the hinged dome and peer into the brooding skull of this extraordinary timepiece.

What we are looking at is a duplicate clock-face, this one placed horizontally. The dial is of mock-ivory with a brass surround. The brass surround is divided into slots marking off the quarter hours. In a baize-lined compartment set into the dome is a supply of tiny ivory tablets.

Now step round to the back of my clock and gaze into the innards. You will observe a pendulum, the usual quota of cogs and wheels, and an ordinary torch battery.

You have seen round the works. Allow me to show you what comes off the production line.

Let's assume that you have a number of engagements in the course of a day – your dentist at one, tea with the Queen Mother at four, cocktails at Number 10 around six-thirty.

You write these appointments in pencil on the ivory tablets provided and place them in the appropriate slots on the horizontal clock-face.

At 12.30 for 1.0 as they say on the invitation cards, an

electric bell rings – PING! – and, like a bar of nut-milk chocolate, the reminder of your first engagement comes tumbling out into the little brass tray. At 3.30 for 4.0 another PING! and an ivory lozenge tells you that it is time to put on your best bib and tucker for the Queen Mum.

Such, at any rate, is the theory. In practice you are likely to be packed off to the dentist at breakfast-time, cocktails with Ted are announced for a quarter-past three, and your brown bread and butter at Clarence House gets mysteriously lost in the works. But we did agree that all clocks are eccentric.

The name of this horological marvel, as announced on the Directions For Management which are pasted up in its brain-box, is THE PATENT AUTOMATIC MEMORANDUM CLOCK. It is vague about its antecedents. I would guess that it started life in Gamage's or the Army and Navy Stores in the nineteen-twenties, the golden age of electrical gadgetry.

Although it has never got me to the church on time my clock, which I think you will now agree is more unique than yours, has provided me with hours of fun. And now I must stop writing about it in the present tense, which is sheer wishful thinking.

Last week it had a brush with an electric kettle. Steam got into its brass-and-ivory nerve centre, the battery began to leak, and my Patent Automatic Memorandum Clock was taken poorly.

It hiccoughed away gently for a few days, sometimes rousing me at four in the morning to remind me that it was time for lunch, sometimes dozing fitfully. Yesterday it coughed up one last feeble message – 'See clock-mender' – and then expired.

I saw clock-mender. He took one look at the God-emperor of alarm clocks and announced that he had never see anything like it in his life, adding for my further information that he never wished to see anything like it again. You could not, he said after the manner of his kind, get the parts.

So I took my clock home again, wrote RIP on one of its ivory tablets, closed its hinged dome for ever and put it away on a high shelf.

I feel quite philosophical about my loss. Time, as Shakespeare reminded us, must have a stop.

Red Sky At Night

Three Russian shepherds, having expressed a wish to set off on a pilgrimage to look for the King of the Jews, are said to have been refused exit visas.

Denying the truth of the story, a Soviet spokesman said that the three men were figments of a fevered Western imagination, that they were all notorious homosexuals and drug-addicts, and that the baby they wished to visit was, behind his swaddling-clothes, a dangerous counter-revolutionary on a par with Trotsky.

He added that the non-existent trio were known to be in league with another gang who were plotting to export gold, frankincense and myrrh without a licence. The whole pack of them were proposing to visit Israeli-occupied territories where many Arabs had been forcibly evicted by Zionists.

Asked what that had to do with the persecution of Jews by the Soviet authorities, the spokesman said that Russia did not persecute Jews and that many of his best friends were Communists.

Refusing to confirm that the three shepherds had been expelled from their union for attempting to emigrate, the spokesman said they had never belonged to the union in the first place. The reason they had been expelled was that they did not know the difference between a sheep and a yak.

Furthermore, he said, they were all highly-qualified agricultural technicians whom a civilised country could ill-afford to lose. If they cared to pay back the £6,000 or so that had been spent on their training, their application would be carefully considered before it was turned down.

Asked how they could raise that kind of money when they had been sacked from their jobs, the spokesman said that that was the way the blini crumbled.

Yesterday the three shepherds learned that they are in danger of being arrested as vagrants. Scotching this rumour, the Soviet spokesman explained that the reason for their arrest was that they were out of work, which is an offence.

Asked how they could get work when the State refuses to employ them, he said that Soviet lambs were too valuable to be tended by vagrants.

He said it was completely untrue that the shepherds would be thrown into prison, where they would be well-treated. No pressure would be put on their wives to divorce them, and the decrees would be rushed through in strict accordance with Soviet law.

If, when they had served their sentences, the three men could prove that they had no criminal record and still wished to emigrate, they would have to get their parents' permission. Told that they had no parents, the spokesman said that regardless of race or creed they were entitled to two apiece.

Asked how a country that calls itself a people's democracy can not only deny its citizens the elementary right to move freely, but imprisons them, reviles, persecutes and humiliates them when they even attempt to do so, the spokesman said that President Nixon's order to renew the full-scale bombing of North Vietnam was an act of naked aggression.

Finally he denied that the three shepherds had been unduly victimised, adding that they were being treated no better and no worse than other Jews who wished to leave Russia. Asked how those Jews were being treated, the spokesman said: 'What Jews?'

The Magic Stocking

I have left it a bit late in the day, but I have decided to initiate a campaign for the Revival of the Christmas Stocking. Your participation is invited.

It seems to me that the Christmas stocking is no longer the institution it was. I put the blame largely on the garment trade, with its passion for changing fashions.

Small boys nowadays wear long trousers and thus short socks. It is easier to pass a pig's ear through the eye of a needle than to make a short sock look like a Christmas stocking.

Small girls wear tights, so that you have the problem either of stuffing both legs with goodies, in which case you might as well use a pillow-case and be done with it; or of filling one leg and wrapping the empty one round it, thus giving the unfortunate child the impression that Santa Claus has left her a haggis.

Parents too have had a hand in the decline of this charming tradition. Instead of according the stocking the respect due to it as a seasonal pleasure in its own right, they have begun to regard their offspring's ankle-wear as a mere extension of the Christmas wrapping paper, into which any small or awkwardly-shaped toy may be shovelled willy-nilly.

This is a sloppy attitude which, if there is to be any enchantment left in childhood, must be stamped out forthwith.

To recap, then. The true Christmas stocking is not a short sock, nor is it a pair of tights, nor is it a dumping-ground for spare torch batteries and ballpoint pens. Nor, for that matter, is it a shop-bought affair of plastic mesh containing nothing but Munchy bars.

What the true Christmas stocking is, we shall now go into in detail. It is not enough to say that it must be knee-length, constructed of wool, and filled to the brim with good things. We are dealing with magic here, and we must be meticulous about our specifications.

As near as I can express it in material terms, a Christmas stocking has got to be nothing more or less than a cornucopia of the five senses.

That is to say, it must first of all satisfy the sense of touch by having many bumps and knobbly bits that may be felt in the dark by small fingers. Then it must satisfy the sense of sight by containing shiny things in bright colours that will dance and glitter by torchlight.

It must satisfy the sense of hearing by emitting a squeaking noise when squeezed and a rattling noise when shaken. It must satisfy the sense of smell, which we will come to in a moment. It must satisfy the sense of taste, which we will come to at once.

The heel-and-toe department of the Christmas stocking must contain a red apple, an orange wrapped in silver paper, a small quantity of nuts and a bag of chocolate pennies. These items are essential. Without them you have not got an authentic Christmas stocking at all, only a cylindrical parcel.

Near the top of the stocking there should be other rations which the junior treasure-hunter may nibble while the exploration gets under way. These may consist of sugar mice, gingerbread men or marzipan pigs, or all three, but they may not consist of Munchy bars.

Now we will deal with the sense of smell. This is very important, for the ideal stocking must smell of Christmas. The smell of Christmas, as I'm sure you remember from your own childhood, is a heady bouquet compounded of the scent of orange peel, marzipan and chocolate mingling with the pungent odour of painted tin.

We have considered the fruit and confectionery side. Let us see what we can do about the painted tin.

Plastic toys, which have no aroma to speak of, have no business in a Christmas stocking. To earn its place in that woolly cave of delights a toy must be a chunky, solid object that feels satisfactorily heavy when handled, and which smells new and exciting when sniffed at.

There are still plenty of corner shops that sell tin toys – clockwork cats that scurry across the lino, tin catherine wheels that give out a rainbow of sparks, tin frogs that make a loud clicking noise when pressed between the fingers. If you cannot get tin, get wood: there is still nothing much wrong with an old-fashioned yo-yo.

A boy, of course, should have a toy trumpet or a mouth organ, a girl should have a small painted doll, and both must have a new torch by which to examine their booty. There will still be plenty of room for completely useless fripperies such as paper fans, Chinese lanterns and cardboard snowmen.

You may think that your children are too old or too sophisticated for such simple joys. I promise you that they are not. There is nothing on Earth to compare with the taste of a sugar mouse eaten at dawn on Christmas morning; and no electric train set or new bicycle will quite match the pleasure of a Christmas stocking that has been filled with thought and care.

What you are giving, you see, is love. And it is the taste and the sight and the feel and the smell and the sounds of love that will always be found in the perfect Christmas stocking.

Speaking Of Words

Professor Alan Ross, who taught us the difference between a serviette and a napkin, is appealing for words and phrases that people find irritating. In a moment I shall offer him some examples from my own extensive collection.

It was Professor Ross, of course, who was responsible for the U and non-U craze that so obsessed this snob-ridden land in the nineteen-fifties. Having your dinner at lunch-time, for instance, is supposed to be very non-U, particularly if you say 'Beg pardon' when the peas roll off your fish-knife.

Why the Professor is collecting those words and phrases is because he is writing a new book that will bring his theory up to date. It seems that even in Mr Heath's one nation you are not socially acceptable unless you go to the lavatory instead of to the W or for a jimmy-riddle-oh; and the Common Market is not so common that you may yet eat preserves in preference to jam.

I've never been sure whether this U and non-U business is an elaborate academic joke or not. Does it seriously bother the upper classes when a non-U mother-to-be says she is 'expecting'? The reason I ask is that it irritates me beyond measure when a U-type expectant mother announces that she is 'preggers', or when I hear that she is 'giving birth' rather than having a baby.

I also object to female university lecturers or research scientists who describe themselves as 'working mums'; to Hampstead mothers who call their children 'the brats'; to the woman who shops in Harrods for prezzies instead of presents; and to all those emancipated *Guardian* readers who have recently acquired boobs in place of breasts.

I don't mind posh persons saying looking-glass when they mean mirror, and I can even accept that they could no more bring themselves to say 'Pleased to meet you' than to spit on the drawing-room carpet. It's the way they were brought up.

What I do mind is the ghastly facetiousness, fake heartiness and bogus self-deprecation with which many upper-crust people now lard their speech. Professor Ross would know better than I why they do it; I would guess they now have a need to sound egalitarian while making it plain that they're still more equal than others.

Whatever the reason, I do not warm to the man who says 'Ciao' instead of good-bye, who sends 'all sorts of messages' instead of his regards, or who says, 'It's only filthy Spanish-type plonk, I'm afraid' when pouring wine.

I cringe at mock-Cockney as used by educated people who call the char-woman 'my lady what does' and who say 'yer actual Chippendale' to apologise for their expensive taste in furniture. I would rather they had straight upper-class migraine than 'one of me turns'.

Another mock-Cockney favourite is 'telly'. If, as Professor

108

Ross would undoubtedly agree, this is a non-U word, why –
along with 'ciggies,' 'cuppa' and 'nosh' – does it become socially
acceptable so long as it is ironically surrounded by verbal quota-
tion marks?

The 'little man' and 'little woman' syndrome is something
else I can do without. U-type wives do not have dressmakers,
they have 'a little woman round the corner'. They do not have
an odd-job man but 'a little man who comes in'. The working
class chap they met on holiday is 'that marvellous little man
from Bootle or wherever'.

U people also have fabulous little grocers, sweet little tobac-
conists and fantastic little wine merchants, thus giving the impression that they are looked after by a race of garden gnomes.
When it comes to professional services, they may well have 'a
funny little Indian doctor' but on the whole they prefer men of
greater stature who have been 'tamed'.

Thus no U-type wife has an ordinary solicitor, she has a tame
solicitor. She doesn't have a dentist like everyone else, she has
'this tame dentist who is absolutely marvellous with kids, I
promise you'.

I could go on all day in this strain – I've just remembered
the very U businessman who charmingly invited me to dinner by
asking if I'd like to try his wife's Chinese throw-up – but as
Professor Ross is a busy man and so am I, we'll leave it at
that.

Probably, anyway, the characters I've been talking about aren't
pukka upper-class at all – just people with a lot of money and a
taste for flowered shirts. They still make my teeth grate. If
there are any words and phrases that irritate you more than
theirs irritate me, I'd be glad to hear about them.

Match Of The Day

Strange encounter in a taxi queue at King's Cross Station.
'Excuse me,' said the man next to me, 'but we seem to be wearing identical shirts. Did you buy yours in Cape Town?'

'No,' I said. 'Marks & Spencers.'

'How very odd,' he said.

As indeed it was, for whereas I was wearing a blue flowered

shirt with a round collar, he was wearing a red-and-white stripe with a pointed collar.

I have been puzzling over this all the week-end, and the only conclusion I can come to is that he did in fact possess a shirt like mine, and thought in a moment of aberration that he was wearing it.

What went through his mind when he got home and happened to glance in the mirror is something I will speculate on for a long time to come.

Crime Does Not Say

Lord Hailsham, for all that he is becoming more pompous as one day succeeds another, presumably knows what he is talking about when he warns us that if the crime figures continue to grow at their present rate, the judicial system will break down.

It doesn't seem much of an answer to suggest, as he did, that what we must therefore do is to restrict the right to trial by jury.

When your house catches fire for the sixth time in succession, the fire brigade may be on good ground in advising you that they are very busy men, and why don't you buy an extinguisher. They would be on better ground if they asked you to find out why the baby is always playing with matches.

What we want to do about crime, surely, is to stop it taking place, rather than to streamline the process of dealing with it so that the courts may get one or two years ahead of the case of Dr Crippen.

I don't see how we can stop crimes happening until we have found out why they happen.

An odd thing about the allied and amalgamated trades of mugging, raping, burglary, vandalism, arson, high treason in Her Majesty's dockyards and robbery with violence is that, considering the sleepless nights they cause us and the vast expense they put us to, we do not know the first thing about them.

I have a sackful of statistics about crime at my elbow as I write. But I have no facts, because there are no facts.

I can give you, in percentages and mean averages, an impressive list of figures concerning – for example – young men who break up railway carriages.

I can tell you how many railway carriages were broken up last month as against the equivalent period in any year since this national sport began; I can give you the proportion of young men caught breaking up railway carriages in 1972 as against those caught in 1971; I can work out their average age and the average sentence they received and the average cost of the damage caused by each one apprehended.

What I cannot tell you, because the information simply does not exist, is why they set out to destroy railway carriages in the first place.

I think we would all sleep easier in our beds if we began to find out.

It seems to me that it is impossible to walk three steps lately without finding yourself in the middle of some official survey or other. I have personally been asked, in the last few months, why I was flying to America (by the Board of Trade); how I liked my new house (by the Environment Department); what I thought about the new canal recreation area (by the local council); and whether I had anything to declare (by HM Customs and Excise).

I have never heard of the Home Office asking prisoners how they came to be in prison.

What happens to a criminal when he gets caught is that he is questioned by the police about what he was doing on the night of the fourteenth; whereupon, with a little encouragement, he may ask for 2,906 other offences to be taken into consideration.

Defence counsel, seeking desperately for some mitigating circumstance that might get him off with a caution, digs out of him some colourful history about the tendency of his mother to breakfast off neat gin. The judge sends him down for seven years and that is the last we hear of him until, in due course, another judge sends him down for fourteen.

Buried away anonymously in the endless columns of Government statistics, you will find this unhappy character occurring and recurring like some recidivist decimal point. But how did he get there? Why does he appear in Table 3 – prison population – instead of Table 168a – self-employed window-cleaners? Nobody knows, because nobody has ever asked.

It has always seemed to me quite absurd that a man can spend seven years, fourteen years, twenty-one years in prison, and when we turn him loose we know no more about him than when we first put him there. The Moors murderers, the railway robbers, the Kray brothers – what do we know about them now that we didn't know on the day they were sentenced? And if we don't want to know, how the hell do we hope to stop others following them?

There are scores of theories about what makes a criminal. Poverty. Personality disorders. Bad upbringing. Bad housing. Bad education. Wrong friends. But in the end, the only one who can tell us how it really happened is the person it's all happened to.

The Home Office, with its genius for making difficulties, would probably say that there are not enough psychiatrists or sociologists available to ask the right questions. I don't see that it's a job for specialists.

Any competent interviewer with a pocket-tape-recorder could build up a fascinating dossier on a prisoner in two weeks. Or even longer, if you like. After all, a man who is serving life has all the time in the world for telling us about what hit him.

The collected biographies of 1,000 convicted criminals would tell us, I suggest, a great deal that we didn't know about the world we've made for ourselves. They might even, in the long run, be instrumental in reducing symptoms of panic in the excitable Lord Hailsham.

Taxing The Brain

My little daughter will be needing a pair of new sandals in April. Will I have to pay Value Added Tax on them?

Not if she eats them in the shop. If she only nibbles at one of the buckles while the shop assistant is trying to make sense of Customs and Excise Notice No. 700, you will have to pay VAT on the unconsumed portion of the sandals.

She is also fond of playing 'Pass the Parcel' at her birthday parties. Does the lucky child who finishes up with the parcel have to pay VAT on it?

Are you joking? EVERYBODY has to pay VAT on the parcel. As each child passes the parcel to the next, it must fill out an input and output voucher and add 10 per cent. However, the last child deducts the output from the input so, technically, nobody pays anything.

What's the big idea, then?

I'm not quite sure. I think 'Pass the Parcel' must be popular in Government circles, too.

Can you explain the difference between output and input in words of one syllable?

That's a pretty fat-headed question, isn't it? Obviously, output is what you pay out and input is what you rake in. No, hang about, though, I'm a liar. It's the other way round. You learn something new every day, don't you?

I am a brewer in a small way and I have a rat in my vat. If I buy a cat to get rid of the rat, will I have to pay VAT?

What on – the cat or the rat? As far as the rat is concerned, it would seem to be nibbling into your output so you can charge it as input. But the rat must provide you with an invoice.

As for the cat, if it eats the rat in the vat, your input will be decreased so you will have to pay VAT on the cat, which becomes output. If the rat eats the cat, your input will have consumed your output so you can claim back the VAT on the cat.

Will I be liable for Value Added Tax on the expense of burying my grandfather?

That depends on whether he is dead or not. If you are burying him just for fun, it becomes entertainment and you must pay VAT at every stage of the enterprise.

However, if your grandfather is actually deceased, and he is turning over in his grave at all this nonsense, and such a turnover exceeds £5,000, he must register immediately for VAT, unless, that is to say . . .

See here, Waterhouse, you haven't the faintest idea what you're talking about, have you?

Not really. Still, I bet I know as much about it as anyone else.

Cat Laugh

In the back streets of Marylebone is a small workshop wherein live two cats – a large black tom and a small ginger kitten.

It is the black cat's habit, after its morning perambulation, to sit on the doorstep miaowing imperiously at passers-by. Those who think it is asking to be stroked are rewarded with an icy stare. It is merely waiting for someone with the simple intelligence to realise that it wants to be let into the shop.

A friend reports that when he passed the shop the other day it was the ginger kitten rather than its black senior that was sitting on the doorstep. Yet the street echoed with the familiar lusty miaowing.

Since the ginger kitten appeared to be gazing serenely into space, he thought for a moment that it had taken up ventriloquism. But when he opened the shop door to let it in, out stalked the big black moggy. It clipped the ginger kitten smartly over the ear and conducted it indoors.

Change For The Worst

The Very Silly Tax scheme, by which shopkeepers are no longer allowed to give change out of a pound note, got off to a smooth start this week.

The object of VST is to eliminate loose change entirely. The trifling increase in the cost of living will be more than offset by the saving on trouser-pocket linings, and the additional revenue raised – it will be collected twice a day by Government lorries – will pay for a new multi-million-pound aeroplane that can fly backwards and say 'Who's a pretty boy, then?'

VST – hailed by Mr Patrick Jenkin, Chief Secretary to the Treasury, as the cutest innovation since tinned grapefruit segments – is devilish in its simplicity.

Basically, it means that nothing in the shops will cost less than a pound. Shopkeepers will have to ring up their transactions on six separate cash registers – one for the original retail price, one for the new price including VST, one for the difference between the retail price and the Very Silly Tax, one for the new VST price minus profit, one for profit minus psychiatrist's fees, and one for luck.

An ingenious system of rounding-up and rounding-down is expected to keep prices level. In many cases it will actually bring them down.

For example, although a box of matches will now cost a pound, so will a ball-point pen previously selling at £1.17. So by purchasing six ball-point pens with every box of matches, it will be possible to get £7.03½-worth of goods for only £7.

A refrigerator priced at £58.49 will go DOWN to £58. But the same refrigerator priced at £58.51 will go UP to £59. So it will pay housewives to shop around. Excursion trains to Aberdeen, Penzance and Juan-les-Pins have been laid on for this purpose.

Treasury officials deny that VST will aggravate inflation. They point out that Moaning Minnies who said the same thing about decimalisation and the Value Added Tax are now having to eat their words. It is true that in many cases, words are all these good people can afford to eat, but that is only because they insist on frittering their money away on shopping.

Weights and measures inspectors touring the shops yesterday said that most traders were operating the new scheme fairly. There were some isolated examples of profiteering – for instance, one Birmingham store was asking £25 for a bar of nut milk chocolate – but this was only because nobody knew what the hell was going on.

Customers who are baffled by the Very Silly Tax are advised to draw all their money out of the bank, hand it to their friendly neighbourhood shopkeeper, and leave the rest to him.

'I am confident,' said the chairman of the VST Board, 'that we can rely on your honest British grocer to play the white man.' He added that in his opinion, the lark was on the wing, the snail was on the thorn, God was in his heaven and all was right with the world.

Level Pegging

What I remember most about school examinations is the smell of blotting paper straight from the stationery cupboard, the taste of the new pen-nib which you had to suck before it would take the ink, and chalk-dust floating up and down the sunbeams.

What I remember least about school examinations is what the hell they were in aid of.

They proved that at a given hour on a given day I could recall

– with the aid of a home-made tattoo on my left wrist, cunningly concealed under an Elastoplast – the names and sources of the principal rivers of Australia. No one asked what I intended to do with the information. I didn't know myself, and I have never had need of it since.

Last week the Schools Council, which is directly responsible for all the dark rings under the eyes of the fifth form at St Dominic's Comprehensive, proposed a reform in the examination system.

The idea is that 'A' levels should be replaced by all sorts of other initials, and that the curriculum should be broadened. The idea is not, unfortunately, that the system should be scrapped completely and rethought from scratch.

The main use of 'A' levels is that you need a batch of them to get a place in a university. If you don't want to go to a university, you still need one or two of them to get you into certain trades. If you don't want to go into those certain trades, they're still handy to show you've been educated.

But educated in what, and as what, and to what purpose? The other day I was chatting to a young man who is swotting away for his 'A' level in English literature. Part of the syllabus is George Orwell's 'Nineteen Eighty-Four' – an enviable assignment, I might say, to one who wasted three terms on 'Julius Caesar', which is probably the most boring play that Shakespeare or anyone else ever produced.

Assuming a mutual interest in the author of 'Nineteen Eighty-Four', I mentioned a couple of other of Orwell's books and wondered if my young friend had read them. Not only had he never heard of them, he had no wish even to take them down from my shelves, and flip through them. They were not, he explained, in the syllabus. Therefore they would be of no use to him in his exam.

I wondered if he knew anything about Orwell's life, which was a fairly interesting one, and proceeded to give him a potted biography. I detected that expression, half desperate, half pitying, which you only see on the faces of young people who are being bored rigid by their elders. Orwell's life was not in the syllabus. There was no need to learn it. There was no *time* to learn it.

It wasn't the first time I'd encountered this lack of curiosity in teenagers. I've known grammar-school girls who could recite

T. S. Eliot backwards, forwards and sideways, but who would have been hard put to identify, let alone quote, any other poet in the English language.

They will sail through their 'A' levels with as much knowledge of the subject they're being examined in as a Derby winner has of the world outside a racecourse. And the fault isn't theirs. It's the fault of the system that teaches them, if teaching is the word.

Originally, the purpose of an exam was to determine how much of the year's work the student had comprehended and retained. Now that notion has been neatly turned on its head. The purpose of the year's work is to determine how many exam questions the student may successfully answer.

The result is that you can leave school with an 'A' level in history and still never have heard, say, of the Industrial Revolution. Even worse, you will have no wish to learn about the Industrial Revolution. Even worse still, if you did have such a wish, you would have no idea how to gratify it. And even worse than that, you would probably be regarded by a Teacher Training College as competent to teach history.

Here's another piece of nonsense. If I wanted to write a column about 'Nineteen Eighty-Four' I would be very silly if I didn't have the book in front of me, as well as my own notes. The young chap I mentioned just now will have to face the same kind of task with nothing more than a ballpoint pen to help him. (I believe one examination board has tried allowing students to refer to the books they've been working from. The educational world is still reeling from this dangerous experiment.)

But if we start on the absurdities of school examinations, we'll be here all day. The main point is that under the system we've got now, they not only discourage real learning, they actively prevent it. Is it really the purpose of 'A' levels to produce a generation of parrots?

Play It With Music

Birthday greetings – for the vast pleasure he has given me over the last thirty years – to Irving Berlin, eighty-five this week-end and the last of the great maestros of Tin Pan Alley.

One of my treasured possessions is a scratchy 78 of the old

tunesmith himself singing one of his lesser-known numbers – 'My British Buddy', which he wrote especially for the London production of his wartime show 'This is the Army'.

'My British Buddy, we're as different as can be,' he trilled in a curiously thin, reedy voice, like some Oxford don doing an audition for the All Souls' panto. *'I like my coffee and rolls and he likes his tea . . .'*

Irving Berlin started his life as a singing waiter in New York's Chinatown. I can testify that if he hadn't made it as a composer he would still be serving chop-suey, with a request from his customers to go easy on the lyrics. (*'When the job is done, and the war is won, we'll be clasping hands across the sea . . .'*)

As well as having written practically every song you have ever heard of – 'A Pretty Girl is Like a Melody', to name only ten – Irving Berlin wrote the tunes for a score of Hollywood musicals – Top Hat, Holiday Inn, White Christmas, There's No Business Like Show Business, Annie Get Your Gun, Call Me Madam.

But though I'm told by the reference books that a 'biopic' of his own life story is on the schedule, no such biopic has ever been made. The reason, I believe, is that Irving Berlin is extremely reticent about his private life being exposed to the public view.

For someone who knows Hollywood as well as he does, this seems a curiously naïve viewpoint. I must have seen just about every Tin Pan Alley musical ever made, from 'The Great Mr Handel' to 'Words and Music', which is alleged to be the story of Rodgers and Hart. Any resemblance between what appears on celluloid and the private life of the subject is purely coincidental.

The Classic Tin Pan Alley musical always starts with two impecunious friends working the agents' offices, trying to sell their songs. This, I agree, puts Irving Berlin at a disadvantage, as there was only one of him. But that's no problem. I'll tell you what, gang – here's a swell column, we could do the show right here . . .

Broadway at the turn of the century. Ike Irving, the son of poor immigrant parents, writes great tunes but terrible lyrics. Bert Berlin, the ne'er-do-well offspring of New York socialites, writes fantastic lyrics but lousy tunes.

As the film opens, they're being thrown out of the offices of Flo Ziegfeld, the great impresario. Bouncing down the steps together, they recollect that they had a fight as children. On the spot, they write 'God bless America' on the back of a used bus ticket and sell it outright for five dollars.

One hit follows another ('Always' . . . 'Cheek to Cheek' . . .). Irving and Berlin have their names in lights. There's some rotten old sub-plot about women – Irving wants to marry and settle down while playboy Berlin wants to go on the town and fritter his money away – but we don't take much notice of that.

Of far more interest is the tune that Ike Irving keeps knocking out on the piano whenever they're short of a number – a tedious march called 'Blankenbauer's German Band'.

Ike Irving thinks that 'Blankenbauer's German Band' is the greatest number he's ever come up with – if only Bert Berlin would write the lyrics. Berlin thinks the song is terrible. They quarrel. Irving goes home to his wife and family. Berlin goes on Skid Row.

One night Bert Berlin is begging for money outside a café on 14th Street. It's snowing and a German band is playing 'White Christmas'. He remembers the song he and his friend wrote in happier times and, brushing aside a tear, enters the café.

Tragedy! The German band is supposed to be appearing in cabaret but, because of the snow, the singer hasn't turned up. Berlin, who cannot pay his bill, offers to sing.

Overcome with remorse, he sings Irving's boring old song, 'Blankenbauer's German and', making the lyrics up as he goes along. The band, which for some reason known only to itself, already knows the tune by heart, goes into ragtime . . .

By a fantastic coincidence, Ike Irving happens to be in the audience. 'Our greatest hit, Bert!' he shouts. 'Blankenbauer's Ragtime Band! If only we had a better title! Listen, I gotta call Flo Ziegfeld right away . . . what's the name of this café?'

'Alexander's.'

If they're not writing songs like Irving Berlin's any more, they're certainly not making films like that any more, which may or may not be a good thing. If they were, though, I bet Mr Bernard Delfont wouldn't be banning them from his cinemas.

Jenny's Birthday

Somewhere in London there is a girl called Jenny. Or, to adjust that statement slightly, possibly not.

Somewhere in Paris, or in Spain, or in Tangier, or in Cornwall, or on the golden road to Samarkand, or perhaps only in the next postal district from where she used to live, there is a girl called Jenny.

I know Jenny as well as anyone can know her – which is to say, not much. She is mercurial; tranquil; impetuous; steady; gregarious; lonely; open; secret; generous and I think she has a small mean streak. In short, an interesting contradiction of herself.

She is a restless, mobile spirit who hankers to grow roots, and a homebody who strikes camp at dawn without leaving a forwarding address for the laundry or her friends. She was in love once.

She is an early riser who gets invited to late-night parties by people who ask for Jen baby. She is a night-owl who is well-acquainted with brisk, efficient secretary-birds who ring her first thing after they have brushed their teeth and ask for Jennifer.

Jen, Jennifer or Jenny has a friend called David who rang her belatedly – several months belatedly – to thank her for the cuff-links.

She has a friend called Bernie who once required her now, this very instant, to come on over and talk about some past misunderstanding. At four a.m.

I don't think David knows about Bernie. I don't think Bernie knows about David. I don't think either of them knows about Harry. We'll come to Harry in a second.

Some of Jenny's friends ring at eight in the evening expecting to find her in. Others ring at half-past midnight and they are not surprised to find her gone.

They never call back, and we'll come to that too. It doesn't much matter, because there are plenty more friends where they came from.

I call them friends because that's what they call themselves, and probably Jenny would fool herself, if she needed them as we sometimes do need friends, that that's what they are. Or were. Acquaintances would be a better word. People she's met. People who don't exist except in other people's address-books, and at other people's parties. And who only come alive when telephones ring.

I know about Jenny because I take a lot of her calls.

She's always been a bit of a roamer but at one point in her life she settled down sufficiently to get a place of her own and probably she shared it with Harry. Or Harry shared it with her, which is more likely, because the telephone was in her name.

She met a great many people and gave them all her phone number. She told them they could ring her day or night, whenever there was any fun going on. Perhaps she told some of them that if Harry answered they'd better hang up the receiver, because that is what some of them still do.

One day for a reason I do not know anything about, Jenny packed her bags and went. To the next postal district. Or Paris, or Spain, or Tangier, or Cornwall, or the golden road to Samarkand. Or back home.

Perhaps she told Harry she was leaving but she didn't tell anyone else – except the Post Office. She said she wouldn't be needing her telephone any more.

The reason I know all this is because when Jenny's line fell vacant, it came to me. And for months and months and months I've been getting her phone calls. At five in the afternoon. Nine in the evening. Midnight. And two, three or four in the morning.

Yesterday, at a respectable hour, a lady called my number and and asked if Jennifer was there.

I said that Jennifer was not.

'Is that Harry?'

I said it was not Harry.

There was the sort of silence that women go into only when they're protecting other women from the consequences of follies that they wish they were committing themselves.

'Did I say Harry? I meant Bernie.'

'No, it's not Bernie either,' I said. 'You've got the right number but the wrong person. Jenny doesn't live here any more.'

'It doesn't matter,' she said. 'I only wanted to wish her a happy birthday.'

Now I'll tell you an odd thing. The phone didn't ring again

yesterday – at least, not for Jenny. Out of all her friends, only one remembered, or knew about or cared about her birthday.

Happy birthday, Jenny. Wherever you are, and whoever you are.

Cost Analysis

Not the most favourite customer of one of my local pubs is the chap who walked in and asked for a glass of their fifteen-pence wine.

'We don't have any fifteen-pence wine.'

'Yes you do – you charge thirty pence a glass for it.'

Midsummer Madness

Midsummer, with all its tricks of light, heat-haze mirages and moonshine revels, is a time of strange encounters.

At any rate, Will Shakespeare got a play out of that proposition, so I'll be damned if I don't get a column out of it.

My first strange encounter was on a hot sombrous midnight in an obscure Northern Line Tube station so deep under the sleeping suburbs that the distant, echoing footsteps sounded like cloven hooves.

There, through the sulphurous fumes, I saw a man writing on the wall.

I agree that such a tableau lacks the magic of, say, a glimpse of Queen Mab flitting through sylvan glades in a cobweb chariot. But my observation of graffiti is that they are apparently self-propagated, appearing overnight like mushrooms. It is not often, in fact it is never, that one sees the graffitist at work.

Emboldened by a good dinner, I endeavoured to add to my wide knowledge of human folly by approaching the owner of the moving hand and asking him why it was writing what it was writing.

In the swirling shadows, a sad white face slowly emerged from a hump of mackintosh. For a wild moment I thought I had stumbled upon the Mock Turtle from Alice in Wonderland.

'What else should I be doing?' demanded an aggrieved, thin voice.

'Well,' I said. 'You could write to your local council, or *The Times*. Or you could go home and listen to the radio or eat a Mars Bar. You could make a model of St Paul's Cathedral out of icing sugar, darn your socks, stand for Parliament, have a cold bath, read a library book or wallpaper the living-room.

'I could suggest many alternatives,' I concluded, 'to writing on walls.'

Through spectacles the thickness of pickle-jars, his small black eyes fixed on me in a mixture of scorn and pity.

'There are homes for people like you,' retorted my felt-tip pen-friend. Then he resumed his handiwork which, when completed, read '*Exterminate all Catholics*'.

My second encounter was a jollier one. On a balmy evening in an English village, when the air was filled with the sonorous buzz of lawn-mowers, I stepped into a pub and asked for half a pint of lager.

Since I had never crossed that particular threshold in my life before, I was a little surprised when the barmaid insisted on doubling my order to a pint and paying for it herself.

'I've got to tell somebody or I'll burst,' she said. 'I had this fellow, see, and we was getting on famous together, but then he goes up north because of his work.

'We lost touch then, but I heard last February that he was back, but he never came near me, never got in touch. Right, I thought, that's that.

'Then, just the minute before you came through that door, he rings me up out of the blue and he wants me to go out with him on Sunday. So you see, there's hope for me yet.'

The barmaid had seen fifty midsummers if she had seen one, her figure was a living testimonial to home-baked bread and suet dumplings, and the sunbeams danced merrily down a roller-coaster of double chins.

She poured my free pint and we drank a toast. To spring in July.

Thirdly, I was returning in the small hours to the West Country hotel where I was spending the night. There was no one at the reception desk but I could see a shirt-sleeved figure smoking a cigarette behind a partition. He could see me too, but he ignored me.

Finally I rapped tentatively on the desk and called: 'Porter.'
Taking his time about it, he approached and I asked for my key.
He took one from the rack and literally threw it in my direction.
When I picked it up I found he had given me the wrong key.
'This is for room 348,' I said. 'I want room 345.'
'You asked for 348,' he said grumpily.
'No I didn't. Why should I ask for 348 when I'm staying in
room 345?'
'You asked for 348,' he snarled. 'And in any case, I'm not
a porter, I'm the banqueting manager.'
'In that event,' I said, 'I'd like a call at 7.30 a.m., and early
morning tea for a hundred and twenty people.'
Lastly, I was driving through Richmond Park last Sunday
when I came across a prodigious traffic jam. Edging my way
forward, I found that a park official was directing the traffic
into a single lane, thus leaving one half of the road free for a
bright green parrot, which was taking a leisurely stroll.

The Magic City

I see that a vacancy has arisen for a city to accommodate
600,000 souls in the neighbourhood of Essex. I hereby apply for
the job of designing it.

If I am not allowed to design it, I may as well warn you what
you will get (assuming that you'll get anything, for despite Mr
Heath's assumption of victory, the battle of Maplin Sands has
not yet even started).

You will get pedestrian tunnels daubed with slogans. You will
get fountains that do not work and promenades on which no
promenading takes place. You will get rust-stained concrete,
piazzas strewn with coke cans, and a sunken traffic roundabout
looking like a gigantic po.

What you will not get is a city, because building cities is
practically a lost art, and very few of us remember the secret.

I will pass on the recipe.

To make a city, you must first take a very large quantity of
good stone from local quarries. With this as your basic ingredient
you fashion a stupendous parallelogram in the Renaissance style,
with Corinthian columns, pilasters, caryatids, gargoyles, balu-

strades, and six great stained glass windows extolling the virtues of commerce, industry, science, agriculture, herring-fishing and the fine arts.

Add marble to taste. Add a mighty organ with 1,500 pipes. Surmount this confection with a dome of copper.

You now have a town hall.

In front of your town hall you must next lay out a flagged square equal in size to a football pitch, and guarded at each corner by stone lions. This square will be dedicated, by a statue on a plinth, to the Unknown Alderman.

You have now built the centre or hub of your city. From this axis you must now cause to be constructed four broad avenues, each equipped with tram-lines. These avenues, which we shall call Corporation Street, Corn Exchange Street, Market Street and Station Road respectively, will conveniently divide your city into quarters.

We will deal with the Corn Exchange Street area first. Taking the remainder of your stone you will first of all build, of course, a corn exchange. To this you will add a number of savings banks, a building society or two, a Conservative Club, a Free Trade Hall, a Philosophical and Literary Society, a cathedral, a parish church, and chapels or tabernacles for the Methodist, Baptist, Unitarian and Four Square Gospel persuasions.

Corpo......on Street will be devoted to civic buildings, including a courthouse, a Department of Sanitation and a mahogany suite of rooms for the truant officer. You must also find space for an infirmary, a public library and museum, an inspectorate of weights and measures and a People's Dispensary for Sick Animals.

Station Road will obviously contain the railway station, together with a solid commercial hotel smelling of gravy. Having taken advice on wind prevalences, you may also place in this quarter your slaughterhouse and your corporation slipper baths.

Now let us build Market Street. Having run out of stone at this stage, we will construct our market hall of glass, and support it on iron pillars encrusted with dolphins. This market hall will be at the centre of a lively bazaar composed of many shops and cafés, an impressive department store, a theatre, several cinemas, and an infinite number of arcades, each one of which will feature an ornamental clock whose hours are chimed by mechanical figures wearing suits of armour.

Drawing our four avenues together, like the strands of a spider's web, there will be an intricate network of back alleys, side-streets and passages. These will house a multitude of small public houses, jobbing printers, pie shops, billiards halls, barbers, engravers and die-stampers, key-cutters, sandwich bars, furtive chemists, knife grinders, fish and chip saloons, painters' sundriesmen and other necessary trades.

Beyond all this, but no farther than a ten-minute tram-ride away, there will be villas and terraces, and semi-detached houses called Dunroamin ; there will be grammar schools and co-operative societies and scout huts and municipal parks; and from every suburban hill we will be able to look down on the spires and domes and twinkling lights of our magic city.

There were such places once, you know. Manchester, Bradford, Birmingham, Leeds, Liverpool, were all such magic cities before they had the guts ripped out of them. They had their faults, God knows, but if they had soot in their lungs they also had red blood in their veins, and there was such a thing as provincial pride.

These places had affectionate nicknames: Cottonopolis, Worstedopolis, Brummagen; and already that unbuilt conurbation in the wastes of Essex has a nickname too: Jet City.

That alone shows that the mould has been broken. There will be no more magic cities.

Advice To A Mollusc

The latest news from Mars is not, as some of us hoped, that it is populated by little green men with TV aerials sprouting from their heads.

All the same, the intelligence to hand is quite intriguing. The hot tip from the red planet is that up there on the other side of the stars, life as we know it is only just on the verge of beginning.

In other words, if the scientists are right (and when did you ever know a scientist to be wrong?) Mars as of August 2, 1973, is in pretty much the same shape as the Earth was 2,000,000,000 years ago.

You will recall, if you cast your mind back, that although

nothing very much was going on at that time, big things were in the offing. So they are on Mars.

An ice cap on that silent planet is going to start shifting and creaking and soon, say in about 500,000,000 years, a new life cycle will be under starter's orders.

When all that remains of the last man on Earth is a flake of white dust in the desert of Kent, the first primeval mollusc will crawl out of some fetid Martian swamp.

It will look around and consider its needs, and after a suitable pause for thought (call it a couple of million years, to be on the safe side) it will begin to develop into something more ambitious than a snail.

It will grow legs, ears, a nose and other appurtenances – all in easy stages. It will find new and amusing ways of reproducing itself. As the centuries roll on and constellations die and the Moon is swallowed up by a black hole in the heavens, Martian brontosauri will stalk the crimson plateaux in the flapping shadows of Martian pterodactyls.

Species after species will originate, evolve, die out, emerge, adapt, combine, coalesce, mutate, engender, propagate, diminish and multiply until at last, when the Earth is but a floating cinder in the sky, some hairy member of the mammalian order of primates will discover that it can stand on its hind legs.

A millennium will pass and then, in a clumsy, arthritic manner, it will close the beginnings of a fist around some object such as a piece of flint.

Another millennium will pass and it will reach out, tentatively, and pluck an apple from a tree. Martian Man will have taken his first giant step.

Towards what?

Towards the bow and arrow, the sling, the blowpipe, the spear, the lance, the sword, the cannon, the musket, the rifle, the hand grenade, the machine gun, the field gun, the anti-tank gun, the anti-aircraft gun, the incendiary bomb, the rocket, the napalm bomb, the atom bomb, the inter-continental ballistic missile, the anti-personnel device, the Molotov cocktail – and the hydrogen bomb.

Towards a six-day war and a seven-year war and a thirty-year war and a hundred-year war, and a thousand civil wars, and an opium war, and a punitive expedition, and a peasants' revolt, and a people's rebellion, and a preventive war, and a massacre of the innocents.

Towards the motor-car, the aeroplane, the tanker, and the juggernaut. Towards the steam train (late), the diesel train (delayed) and the electric train (cancelled). Towards the tram-car in all its versions, and the trolley-bus. Towards the long queue for the non-arrival of the double-decker bus.

Towards a plundering of the mountains and a befouling of the seas, a squandering of minerals and a polluting of the rivers. Towards industrial waste, oil slicks, smog, slag heaps, DDT, strontium 90, carbon monoxide and effluent of potash.

Towards thalidomide and other discoveries.

Towards nerve-gas.

Towards thrombosis, syphilis and hatters' madness.

Towards slum houses and slum schools, inadequate pensions, old women eating cardboard, low wages, high prices, great profits and silly taxes. Towards computers, motorways and pneumatic drills.

Towards greed and vanity and lust: towards murder, rape, arson, vandalism, and robbery with violence. Towards the bankruptcy of architects, the follies of politicians, the peccadilloes of disc jockeys and the major misdemeanours of presidents.

Towards inquisition and torture. Towards treachery and betrayal. Towards hanging from a cross on a green hill.

My advice to the Martian mollusc: stay in that swamp.

Ales In The Dales

Ilkley Moor, we are asked to believe, is wearing out. Countless legions of walkers, not to mention generations of Mary Janes doing their courting, have reduced great tracts of it to bare rock.

If there's a fund for patching up that rolling purple quilt with re-tread heather, I'd better subscribe. I must have worn out a broad acre or two in my time.

I was going to say that I wouldn't mind having a pint for every mile I've tramped across Ilkley Moor. But come to think of it, I *have* had a pint for every mile I've tramped across Ilkley Moor. There must be few West Riding men who haven't.

For southerners and other outcasts who sip weak tea out of

paper cups on the edge of their allegedly rolling downs, I had better explain that Ilkley Moor was not constructed for tee-totallers. To savour it to the full you need hollow legs, dubbined boots, a compass, an ordnance survey map and a liver like a bicycle saddle.

It is also an advantage to be settled in your ways.

Restive spirits may discover a thousand gusty delights on Ilkley Moor: becks and rills and druids' circles; mists and fogs, and clouds that brush their shoulders; golds and purples; curlews, waterfowl and plovers; wild campion, forget-me-not and mountain flowers. They may imagine themselves one minute to be in Greenland; the next, and they are looking down a valley at a nest of mill chimneys.

Only those of settled ways, however, find themselves outside the right door at opening time.

The ritual of Ilkley Moor is observed on Saturdays, Sundays and Bank Holidays, but as far as I know it is not yet compulsory. Arriving at the traditional meeting point, a crop of murderous rocks called the Cow and Calf – which resemble, incidentally, neither cows, calves, nor any other form of animal life still extant – you are theoretically as free as the common snipe to go in any direction you please. You can, if you so wish, head for the Pennines and finish up at Hadrian's Wall.

But for the true connoisseur, there is only one path. Proceeding through a Khyber Pass of crags you climb from one ling-and-bracken horizon to another until you think the sky cannot be far off. Then, with the salt air stinging your cheeks and a wind that seems to sing through your veins, you take your bearings.

There below you, so far away that it might be in Derbyshire, is a toy-town rooftop.

Negotiating a few cairns, falling into a stream or two, and avoiding the tempting green sheep-track to the left that will lead you straight into a bog, you follow the pilgrim's way ever downward. When the pilgrim's way peters out, as it frequently does, you keep that small rooftop in your line of vision. When the rooftop vanishes behind a yellow bluff of gorse, you follow your nose.

Given luck and a good breeze behind you, you will eventually reach some hill-pastures and, beyond them, a stile. Descending a narrow gully that is path or waterfall according to the season,

E   129

you will ultimately attach your rooftop to four bare walls. The completion of the jigsaw will establish an inn that clings precariously to the far edge of the moor.

This is Dick Hudson's, which may justifiably claim to be the most famous pub in all Yorkshire, or indeed the world. Nowhere does a glass of Tetley's ale taste so good as when you have completed that two-hour trek over the brow of Ilkley Moor – or 'ovver t'top' as we say up there.

A second glass puts you in just the right frame of mind for a third, and if you fancy a plate of boiled ham or a bit of Cheshire cheese and a slice of onion in a brown teacake, that too can be arranged. For afters, before you attempt the return sortie and discover that, contrary to the teachings of Euclid, it is uphill both ways, the Scotch is recommended.

There may be Yorkshiremen who did not learn their drinking at Dick Hudson's, but if so I have never met them. You start young, with a glass of lemonade and a packet of crisps in the pub garden after your first youth-club hike along the nursery slopes.

Graduating to halves of shandy, you escort a succession of protesting girl-friends 'ovver t'top', assuring them that there is only one more mile to hobble in their unsuitable shoes. As a young man, you guzzle your first pint greedily; as an older, wiser one, you sip thoughtfully, serene in your faith that there is plenty more where that came from.

It is perfectly possible to reach Dick Hudson's by car or bus, I have seen people doing it – foreigners, mainly Lancastrians – people of that calibre. A West Riding man, though, with his Methodist conviction that pleasures have got to be paid for, would think himself soft if he tackled his Sunday morning pint without that two-hour route march across the moors.

What parts of Ilkley Moor are wearing thin the reports don't say. I should be surprised, though, if there weren't a few bald patches between the Cow and Calf rocks and Dick Hudson's.

The Sweet By-and-by

Do not send to know for whom the bell tolls. It tolls for the gobstopper, the aniseed ball and the sherbet dab.

The muffled clapper also knells for the pear drop, the acid

drop, the lemon drop and the liquorice bootlace, and for all forms of slab toffee which the shopkeeper breaks with his little hammer.

The funeral address was read at the week-end by one of the courtiers of the confectionery kingdom.

Traditional sweets, he lamented – although I notice that he did not anoint himself with boiling humbug-mixture in his grief – have had it. They are no longer an economical proposition.

Well now, that depends on which side of the counter you are standing.

A penn'orth of aniseed balls in a three-cornered paper bag used to see me through the Tom Mix serial, the Mickey Mouse cartoon, the Three Stooges, the Pete Smith speciality, the Laurel and Hardy, and the trailer for next week's Superman. Whereas a four-and-a-half-pence bar of Scrumpo in its glossy wrapper barely lasts through the twenty-second commercial for the same bland product.

If all sweet manufacturers were seven years old they would know what was an economical proposition all right. Everlasting toffee is an economical proposition. All-day suckers are an economical proposition. Stickjaw, blackjack and treacle toffee are economical propositions.

But although it pays to buy such fondly-remembered goodies it does not pay to sell them. Market research, that business equivalent of Chase the Ace, Find the Lady and other three-card tricks, shows that what the customer wants nowadays – or to put it another way, what the customer will get – is a pre-wrapped, pre-weighed, commercialised, advertised, anaesthetised tube of glump.

If they thought they could get away with wrapping gob-stoppers in fancy paper and packaging them in boxes of twelve to be sold in cinema foyers, you may be sure that not only would the gobstopper still be with us, but some celestial sweetmeat choir would be singing gobstopper jingles on TV. ('*Gobstoppers are just the job . . . Gobstoppers stop your gob . . .*').

But perhaps we should not sob overmuch into our redundant lucky bags – Lucky bags! Dolly mixtures, bubble-gum, a whistle, a puzzle, some transfers, a balloon and three toffees, all for a penny! – for the obituaries may have been premature.

After all, it is only the big combines that are rationalising themselves out of the all-day sucker market. I am sure that in many back-street factories, as likely as not infested with rats, the aniseed-ball cauldron bubbles on and the gobstopper foundry is still operating at full pelt. Long may they flourish.

The trouble with the big boys is that while they can produce a perfectly adequate after-dinner mint that gets passed round the table like port, they have no understanding of a child the height of three marzipan teacakes, clutching a penny.

In my local sweetshop the other day I saw a packet of jelly babies. Now a boy of three could tell those responsible for this transgression that you do not put jelly babies in packets. You buy them loose and put them in pockets, and with any luck they come out covered in fluff.

There is far more to a sweet than the eating of it. The perfect sweet not only melts in the hand, it melts whenever it is exposed to daylight – on frocks and shirt fronts, on occasional tables, clean towels, radio sets, library books and unread newspapers, on the underside of school desks – and liberally around the lips.

The perfect sweet is round in shape and hard in texture. It can be fielded as a substitute in a game of marbles or used as an offensive weapon.

Among the functions of the perfect sweet is to dye the tongue vermilion or stain the teeth black. Ideally, it should change colour when removed from the mouth for inspection. It should lactate juices that can squirt an enemy in the eye at three paces. It should be divisible among friends. It should make a satisfactory noise when sucked and an even more satisfactory noise when crunched. It should attract fluff.

Above all, it should be available in large quantities for the smallest coin in the realm. If manufacturers can no longer afford to produce it, then governments should subsidise it, and put a swingeing tax on the tubes of glump which are impertinently trying to replace the perfect sweet, the model gobstopper, the impeccable all-day sucker.

The Good Companion

I cannot remember how old I was when I seized this particular great thick book from the returned-fiction shelves of the public library.

Eleven or twelve, probably. I had tired of Biggles and the William books by then and, on the authority of my grown-up sister's library ticket, was attempting a cautious toehold on adult reading.

The returned-fiction shelves, I quickly learned, was where the fat catches were made. There I met Arnold Bennett, H. G. Wells, G. K. Chesterton, Evelyn Waugh – and this particular great thick book.

I do remember, very well, scurrying home through the January sleet with the treasure tucked inside my top coat. I remember sitting by the fireside with my socks steaming and a milky skin forming over my untouched cup of cocoa, and the great thick book open on my mottling knees.

I remember the wizardry of the opening paragraph:

'There, far below, is the knobbly backbone of England, the Pennine Range. At first, the whole dark length of it, from the Peak to Cross Fell, is visible . . .'

I quoted that at first from memory and then, checking with the battered old original – first published in 1929, the year I was born – found that I had got only three or four words wrong. Not bad. But not all that good, considering that I have been reading it annually for the best part of thirty years.

The book, of course, is 'The Good Companions'. The author is J. B. Priestley. He enters his eightieth year this week, and this is my birthday card.

Can't you still see Jess Oakroyd on his way home from the Bruddersford United ground?

'Something very queer is happening in that narrow thorough-fare to the west of the town . . . What is so queer about it now is that the road itself cannot be seen at all. A grey-green tide flows sluggishly down its length. It is a tide of cloth caps.'

But already I can see the old man tapping his pipe impatiently – primarily, I should think, at being called an old man; for although J. B. Priestley has frequently experimented with Time, Time's experiments with J. B. Priestley have not yet put him into his dotage. And secondly, at my rambling on about 'The Good Companions', which is like telling Charles Dickens that 'The Pickwick Papers' was very good or reminding Olivier that he was a great Hamlet.

Priestley could have made his reputation a dozen times over with his other novels, and if he hadn't, there were a dozen reputations to be made anyway. As a dramatist (from 'When We Are Married' to 'An Inspector Calls', now enjoying a well-deserved revival); as an essayist, critic, broadcaster (those war-time 'Postscripts'), biographer, screenwriter (fifty points if you remember Tommy Trinder in 'The Foreman Went to France') – or simply as Jolly Jack, the scourge of Admass and equivalent nonsenses.

If he had written only 'English Journey', my copy of which is even more well-thumbed than 'The Good Companions', it would have been enough.

I am not, thank God, a literary critic, and those damned souls who are literary critics have always been wary of Priestley. He has written far more than the restrictive practices of English Literature permit, and what is worse, he has done so in language that the common man can understand. That is unforgivable.

But if I were a literary critic, and you were to ask me to state in a few paragraphs why J. B. Priestley's birthday is worth celebrating with bells and fireworks, I'll tell you what I'd say.

He is the last of a great line of authors who knew how to teach their readers. That's why I bracketed him with Wells, Chesterton and Bennett.

Writers don't teach nowadays. They don't even try to reach the ordinary man. They write about problems of identity for people who can afford to worry about such matters. With the price of books today, they probably know their audience.

Priestley belongs to a fast-dying breed of writers who wanted to tell people things. People like myself, who came out of school half-literate, could learn from them. I can still learn from Priestley.

He can make you think. He can make you laugh. He is not ashamed to make you cry, and you are not ashamed to do so when he works the trick.

He can make you look at old things in a new way, and what is perhaps more important, he can force you to look at new things in the old way. He can make you ponder a little about what you're up to.

He writes, incidentally, like an angel.

Happy birthday, J. B. Priestley.

Do You Remember?

I had this riveting experience. I happened to remark that someone reminded me of Tommy Handley and the man I was with –
by all the evidence an adult person of mature years – said:
'*Who's Tommy Handley?*'

It's possible that if you're under the age of 25 you won't know
what I'm talking about either. In which case you'll probably
remain bewildered for the rest of this piece. Away to the discotheque with you and I hope you break your leg.

The rest of my audience, I hope, will sympathise with one
who is in the throes of his fortieth year. I've been in this
traumatic state for seven months now and still haven't got over
it. Somebody told me the other day that you'll never feel so old
again as when you're 40. I sincerely hope that's true. Golden
youth has disappeared like a sunset and you suddenly notice
there really is a brick wall between the generations.

Have you ever tried explaining to a six-year-old boy what
trams used to be? Or to a 14-year-old what a Sunderland flying
boat looked like?

Do you remember silver threepenny bits? Lucky bags? Stiff,
oblong bus tickets with holes punched in them? Third-class
railway carriages? *Monday Night at Eight?* ARP? Pip, Squeak
and Wilfred? Stop me and buy one?

Do you remember indelible pencils that made your tongue
purple when you licked them, gramophone records that broke
when you dropped them? Cigarette cards and Shirley Temple
lollipops? Do you remember going into the tobacconist's and
asking if he'd any Wild Woodbines, and when he said yes you
retorted 'Well tame them!' and ran? Score 80 per cent and you're
probably on my side.

I've only realised recently – seven months and fourteen days
ago, if you want it in figures – that I've been going through my
life under the delusion that I was a very young man. I was one
of those people who kept on the ball. Peter Pan wasn't in it. No
one was more at home in the King's Road, no one was more
permissive about pot smoking, I knew what was in the Top
Twenty, and I could do the Twist. (The Twist! It sounds like
the Black Bottom.)

One thing I was never going to do and that was bore the
bell-bottoms off the younger set about the good old days. When

I was a child the world seemed to be full of people like that. They used to tell us over and over and over again how for sixpence they were able to get a seat at the music hall, a four-course dinner, a bottle of stout and five cigarettes, and still have change for a cab-ride home.

How I went off beam I'm not quite sure. I remember my fortieth birthday. I remember thinking that it wasn't as bad as all that – I still had my own teeth and my own hair, and I could understand practically every word that Tariq Ali said. Then, as if in a dream, as if it was somebody else speaking, I heard myself telling my son that when *I* was a lad we only got a penny a week pocket money, and you could buy a strip of everlasting toffee and still have a ha'penny left when the sarsaparilla man came round.

It was as if my forty candles had called up a sleeping demon – I could feel, as if I were being physically dragged backwards, this definite pull towards the past. I began to sentimentalise about things I couldn't possibly remember – airships, horse drawn funerals, the Jarrow march. And about a lot of things I honestly could remember: Tom Mix, whip and top, farthings, Neville Chamberlain's umbrella, barrage balloons, weighed-out butter, Stainless Stephen – and saying 'Abyssinia' when you meant goodbye. But it didn't matter whether I really recalled these things or not. The main object was to identify myself, willingly and voluntarily, with a world that was dead and buried.

Why the hell do we do this? Why do we talk as if the world had come to an end when they pulled up the tram-lines and took off *Band Waggon*? (Remember Nausea Bagwash?) It's a kind of suicide when you think about it – a deliberate contracting-out of life as it's lived today and, therefore, since today is where we all find ourselves, a rejection of life itself.

A psychiatrist, especially if he's a youthful psychiatrist, would tell you that we brood on the past because we're jealous of the young. But I think for a lot of middle-aged people – who after all don't honestly go puce with rage when they have the great fortune to see a girl in a see-through dress – there's a less sophisticated reason.

They hark back to bygone days because they felt a damn sight more in touch with things then than they do now. The only benefit of age is experience, and what's the good of experience when large chunks of it are becoming obsolete by the minute?

What was the good of all those dancing lessons when the foxtrot has suddenly become an old-time dance? What's the use of knowing how to change the nib in your Blackbird fountain pen when they've gone and invented ballpoints?

Look at the conglomeration of useless knowledge in your attic of a mind: the names of LMS crack expresses, the words to Henry Hall's signature tune, the result of the 1934 Test Match, the quickest way to the Holborn Empire, the price of Black Cat cigarettes before the war – and who wants to hear your imitation of Adolf Hitler now? What's the use of having mastered boogie-woogie?

It isn't youth that's the enemy, it's progress. But if you do feel jealous of the young ones, you might get some vicious pleasure out of contemplating that they've got it coming to them, too. It doesn't matter how with-it or groovy they are, or what their scene might be – they can wear the latest 'in' worry-beads for the rest of their lives and they'll still wake up one morning and wonder what happened to black and white television.

They'll remember pre-decimal coinage, and telephone exchanges with funny names like MAYfair, FRObisher and TEMple Bar. They'll remember suspender belts, hula hoops, the last steam trains, milk bottles, unwrapped bread, gear levers on cars, spy films, censorship and Radio Caroline. They'll feel extremely old. And *that*'ll teach them to ask me if the Jitterbug was a flying bomb.

A happy birthday to all my readers.

Laughing Gas

I understand from those who have gone through the experience that when you are converted to natural gas, you go mad.

I believe it. The arrival of the Gas Board Crazy Gang in my street has already qualified me for the laughing academy – and I don't even have gas.

It would have been kinder if they'd simply turned up with a strait-jacket and bundled me into the plain van. Instead, they have chosen a process somewhat akin to the Chinese water torture.

It started a few weeks ago when a procession of officials,

like heralds in a village pageant, began to canvass the neighbour-hood with tidings of comfort and of joy. Natural gas, they announced, was on its way.

When I told them I was all-electric they looked disappointed, wrote the sad news down in their Domesday Books, and went away. This did not prevent a further procession of officials – this lot with the fervour of Crusaders entering the gates of Jerusalem – arriving to tell me that the glad day was about to dawn.

I asked them what glad day, and they said the glad day when I would be converted to natural gas. I told them that the way I was situated, they would find it easier to turn base metal into gold, and they too went away.

Last week a travelling circus of vans, trucks and trailers moored itself in the street. And the doorbell rang.

'Good morning. Do you have gas?'

No. As I believe I have already mentioned to half a dozen of your colleagues.

'No gas at all?'

I wasn't sure how I was expected to answer that one. 'Well, just a tenny-weeny little gas,' perhaps. Or: 'Now that you men-tion it, I do recollect that I have gas-fired central heating, a gas cooker, a wash-boiler, sixteen gas fires, and my own private gasometer in the back yard.'

No gas at all, I said.

'You have no gas appliances of any description whatever?'

Only the 1,800 horsepower regenerative-cycle gas turbine in the loft, I felt like saying. Aloud, I confirmed that I had no gas appliances of any description whatever.

The Doubting Thomas of North Thames finally departed, and I settled down to some work. Half an hour later I was going through the whole litany again with Doubting Thomas Mark II, who seemed to think that if only I racked my brains I would remember putting some gas away for a rainy day.

The following morning I was not persecuted at all, and I thought the message had finally got through. And so, in a way, it had: for in the afternoon a very understanding chap from the Gas Board turned up to say that since I wasn't being converted, he had better cut off my gas meter.

'I don't have a gas meter,' I said, adding that there was a sound reason for this discrepancy. I didn't have gas.

'All the same,' he said, 'I'd better check.'

'Check what?'

'That you don't have a gas meter.'

'And how would you propose to set about doing that?'

'Well – by looking for it, I suppose.'

'Let me get this clear,' I said. 'You want to come in and search for something I haven't got, which, since it doesn't exist, could be anywhere in the house. Where do you want to look first – in the broom-cupboard or under the bed?'

He seemed to concede that there was a certain warped, twisted logic to my argument. 'I'll tell you what I'll do,' he said. 'I'll make a note on your card that you don't have gas.'

'You do that little thing,' I said.

I had no sooner closed the door than the bell rang again and I found myself face to face with two men in white coats. This is it, I thought – they've come for me at last. But no, they only wanted to look at my gas cooker.

Bottled Boyhood

If I were a responsible citizen I should be urging you to do as the man says and yield up your empty milk bottles.

Pretty silly we shall look, after all, if milk has to be rationed not because there is a shortage of cows, and not because the glass-blowers are running out of puff, but because 547,000,000 bottles a year are posted missing.

There, I'm afraid, is where my magpie mind reveals its anti-social partiality for unconsidered trifles. Scrub round the milk crisis, I hear myself saying – what interests me is the purpose to which that astronomical quantity of absentee bottles is being put.

What the dairies are up against in this campaign of theirs is that in this country the milk bottle has always been popularly regarded as a legitimate buckshee artifact – which the dictionary defines as an object made by man with a view to subsequent use.

At least it was so when I was a lad, and the subsequent uses were legion.

Nowadays, I'm not so sure. Round my way the secondary fate of empty milk bottles is to be kicked into basement areas by

139

mischievous boys. But thirty years ago, if you had asked us for roll-call of 547,000,000 missing milk bottles, we could have accounted constructively for every last one of them.

One hundred million of them would have contained acorns, from which their custodians would have erroneously believed that mighty oaks would grow.

A further 100,000,000 would have been commandeered as flower vases for bruised little posies of bluebells, buttercups, cowslips, dandelions or, at a stretch, deadly nightshade.

Fifty million, furnished with duvets of cabbage-leaf, would have been converted into hostels for furry caterpillars.

Seventy-five million would be half-filled with earth, and in that earth would be planted, in equal ratio, 75,000,000 orange pips, lemon pips and grapefruit pips. These were expected to develop into luscious fruit groves alongside the mighty oaks. Another 75,000,000 would have been used as test-tubes in backyard laboratories. See my paper, *The effect on molten lead-piping when tipped out of a red-hot Oxo tin into a milk bottle full of cold water*, written in Leeds Infirmary in 1937.

Sixty million would accommodate frog spawn or home-made liquorice juice, or both.

Ten million bottles would contain lighted candles, and to the necks of each of those 10,000,000 bottles would be tied a rope, and if you could swing your bottle round your head without the candle going out, you were a better man than I was.

Thirty million would be employed as thawing-out chambers for dried-up paintbrushes, until the bristles snapped off altogether, when they would be used as catapult targets.

As well as being able to account for 547,000,000 milk bottles, by the way, we could equally have accounted for 547,000,000 milk bottle tops. We collected 'em.

The milk bottle tops you got in that age of waste-not-want-not were nothing like the rubbishy tinfoil medallions you see today. They were flat, cardboard jobs with a circular bit in the middle that you pressed out in order to open the bottle. When you had wiped the milk out of your eye, you were left with an extremely useful device.

You could do all manner of things with these bottle-tops. You could thread a string through them and wear them round your neck like a Hawaiian aloha-wreath. You could wind raffia around them and make raffia-covered bottle-tops. You could wedge them in your mouth and stick your tongue, hideously contorted, through the hole in the middle.

Or, you could, as many of us did, save them in vast numbers and take them to school in the belief that a billion milk-tops would provide a seaside holiday for a poor old lady. (I see from Iona and Peter Opie's *The Lore and Language of School-children* that this myth, in various forms, goes back at least to the 1850s, and that it still flourishes.)

Speaking of school, I find that I've left 47,000,000 empty milk-bottles unaccounted for. Well, that's where you would have found them – in school, all lined up on the radiators and window-sills of the nature class. And each one would contain a crocus bulb, hopefully to take root, flourish and bloom beneath the orange, grapefruit and lemon groves, in the shade of those mighty oaks.

And now enough of this subversive talk. Give your empties back to the milkman at once, and don't forget to tip out the tadpoles.

Tea Break

There is a great rambling hotel in Blackpool which is renowned for its amiable inefficiency. A sure way of getting bacon and eggs for breakfast is to order a kipper.

It is also renowned for its inability to cope with unusual circumstances – for example, the arrival of a guest.

One afternoon this week I asked if I could have some tea in my room. The following dialogue ensued:

Desk clerk: Sorry – no room service.

Me: But I had tea in my room this morning. Or rather I didn't, because it never arrived, but I certainly ordered it.

D.C.: Yes – but we only serve tea with an early call.

Me: Then could I have an early call for 4.30 p.m.?

I didn't get it, but I felt better.

Trouble In Store

Harrods, you may have seen in the papers, may be taken over by Boots. On Saturday, I wished it had been taken over by an earthquake, and although it causes me pain to do so, I will tell you why.

I was mooning about in this elegant emporium when I came across my eldest daughter doing her Christmas shopping.

Now there are only two things to be done when you come across your eldest daughter doing her Christmas shopping. You can either steal quietly away, for fear of catching her in the act of choosing you a tie, cigar-cutter or pair of gloves; or you can sneak up behind her, prod her in the small of the back with two fingers, and exclaim 'BANG!'

Since I had encountered my eldest daughter in the toy department, where it seemed unlikely that she was buying me a doll's house, I selected the latter course.

What eldest daughters do when they have been prodded in the back to the accompaniment of the expression 'Bang!' is to turn round. And, of course, when she did turn round it wasn't her at all.

Now this is the kind of situation that anyone might find himself in while mooning about in Harrods, or, for that matter, Marks and Spencer or Debenham and Freebody's. The usual drill is to blush to the roots of your hair, explain to the total stranger you have just accosted that you had mistaken her for your eldest daughter, and shamble away, closely watched by the store detectives.

But these circumstances were not usual. By one of those fortuitous coincidences that make life unbearably interesting, this was not a total stranger at all but a woman I knew slightly.

I had, in fact, met her only once before, but on that occasion – for reasons which you are about to drag out of me, although I would sooner forget the whole thing – she formed the impression that I was a certifiable lunatic.

Let the years roll back to 1970 – or it may have been 1969, who cares? I am at a very large and rather boring reception in London. I have been cornered by a lady who insists on telling me, at some length, about the book she is writing.

In due course she asks me what I do for a living. I am reluctant to confess that I also am in the writing game. So naturally I tell her that I am the general manager of a large chimney-sweeping concern.

I am just informing this lady about the success of my revolutionary vacuum process on the left-hand-thread spiral chimney to be found only in Norfolk when she is joined by her escort.

Her escort turns out to be an old friend of mine.

As I make my excuses, and leave, I hear the unmistakeable hysterical laughter of an old friend who has just been told that I am very knowledgeable on the subject of chimney-sweeping.

Mercifully – although I knew for a certain fact that she was putting it about London that I was off my chump – the paths of that lady and mine have not since crossed.

Until Saturday.

I would like you now to put yourself in her place.

She is browsing innocently through the toy department of Harrods, perhaps wondering whether Lego or a Spirograph would best suit her favourite nephew. Suddenly she feels an excruciating pain as two fingers prod her in the back. Simultaneously, a gruff baritone voice remarks: 'BANG!'

She jumps. She turns. She stares. And she discovers that the madman is still at large.

Can you wonder that, in the middle of a crowded department store, she shied back as if confronted by a rapist on a lonely towpath?

Can you wonder that, when my mouth opened, no words came out?

Can you wonder that, when speech was magically restored, I listened in horror at my own disembodied voice? 'Well,' I heard myself babbling. 'So here we are again.'

Can you wonder that I wished Harrods and everybody in it would be swallowed up by an earthquake?

Uncles Unanimous

One of my abiding regrets about the Christmases of my boyhood is that I did not have enough uncles.

It is well-known that the more uncles you can cram into a front room at Christmas time, the merrier that front room will be. As Dylan Thomas explained in his enchanting essay, 'A

Child's Christmas in Wales', 'There are *always* Uncles at Christmas.'

There must be other ingredients, of course: the holly and the paper-chains, the tree, the presents, the box of 'Eat Me' dates, the cards that tumble from the mantelpiece, and the second layer of chocolates with a nest of shredded paper where the montelimar ought to be.

And the mistletoe held precariously by a drawing-pin; and a silver coin in each portion of Christmas pud, where, by all the rules, there should be only one in the whole boiling; and the frantic search for the nutcrackers; and the whole house drenched in the smell of tangerines.

But above and beyond and in addition to all these and other good things, there should be an abundance of uncles.

There should be uncles of all shapes and sizes; fat uncles who burp and chuckle and drink bottled beer all through the Royal broadcast; thin uncles with dyspeptic faces who can tell deadpan jokes and do conjuring tricks with pennies; burly uncles, built like Glasgow trams, who can hold a wriggling nephew up to the ceiling on one beefy palm while cracking a walnut in the other; youthful uncles who tickle the same wriggling nephews into hysteria; old uncles, as wizened as grandfathers, whose owlish wink contains the promise of half a crown; small, shiny uncles in celluloid collars, who can eat their own weight in pork pies.

There should be . . . but what is the collective noun for uncles? A joviality of uncles? A corporation of uncles? A rumbling of uncles? A riddle-me-ree of uncles? A tickling of uncles? A chucking-out-time of uncles?

At any rate, there should be uncles in quantity; and in my street – although regrettably not in my house – there were always so many uncles on Christmas Day that if they had decided to fight the Battle of Mons all over again (as they might well have done, the way they used to argue about it) they could have formed an Uncles' Battalion of the King's Own Yorkshire Light Infantry.

They came in two waves the early shift and the late shift.

The early shift arrived in the street soon after breakfast, with leatherette carrier-bags that clanked and rattled, and a mysterious package or two, and ill-tied parcels containing unplucked turkeys and perhaps a blue cabbage from the allotment. These were the ones who had come for their Christmas dinner, and they were not much use after it.

Again to quote Dylan Thomas: 'After dinner the Uncles sat in front of the fire, loosened all buttons, put their large moist hands over their watch chains, groaned a little and slept.'

But not all uncles. In Yorkshire, if not in Wales, there was the second shift yet to come.

The second shift loomed into view when Christmas dinner was over, or after the pubs had closed, whichever was the later; and although they usually came empty-handed – having left their parcels in the saloon bar – they were far more fun. They were a swaying of uncles, a shouting of uncles, a singing of uncles; they were the uncles of childhood mythology, stepping miraculously, for one day only, out of the pages of Film Fun and the Rainbow Annual.

These uncles had watches on gold chains, with a secret door at the back that would spring open to reveal the works; they had waistcoat pockets stuffed with shillings, which they would hand out at random to any boy in sight, with advice not to spend it all at once; they had fat cigars; they had peppermints; they had snuff-boxes which they would let you sample – and your sneezes would set their chins (they had several each) a-wobbling like the untouched Christmas jelly.

They had a repertoire of anecdotes and a fund of inscrutable sayings; and soured spinster aunts and faded widowed mothers who did not smile from one year's end to another would dissolve into helpless mirth at their tricks. They could do other wondrous things, too.

The boy two doors up had an uncle who could sing 'A-tisket, a-tasket, I've lost my yellow basket' backwards, with a glass of water balanced on his head. The boy two doors down had an uncle who could drink a pint of beer while standing on his hands. The boy across the way had an uncle who could pull the cloth from under a laden tea-table, without accident, nine times out of ten. And as the street grew dark on those Christmas afternoons, the booming avuncular laughter echoed like the thunder of the gods.

I have explained that my uncles were thin on the ground. There were too few of them, and they lived too far away for me to enjoy the annual festive union of uncles except as a fascinated observer.

But there was a year, just one, when I had my own Christmas uncle, and I have never forgotten it.

It was a Christmas Eve, rather than the more proper time of Christmas Day, when this uncle arrived. I was about seven or eight – old enough (in those innocent days) to be left alone in the house – 'minding the fire' as we called it – while my mother was shopping.

The knock that almost rattled the tiles off the roof was undoubtedly an uncle's knock. The beaming figure on the doorstep was unquestionably an uncle: and a swaying, second-shift uncle at that. He held in one large paw a shiny, brightly-painted toy wheelbarrow, from which the sodden corrugated-cardboard wrapping was falling away in shreds. A Christmas present, he explained, for his favourite nephew.

I told him that my mother was out but he did not seem unduly concerned. He sang me a little song, gave me three pennies fresh from the mint, waggled his false teeth up and down, counselled me to be a good lad, and departed.

I had never seen him before and I have never seen him since, but he was an uncle all right. I could tell uncles a mile off.

But the odd thing is this. I forgot to ask his name and he forgot to tell me it; but later, in response to a questionnaire from my mother, all known uncles denied having rolled up at the house that night, presenting their favourite nephew with a wheelbarrow and singing little songs, much less waggling their false teeth.

My mother concluded that he wasn't a real uncle at all and warned me against opening the door to strange men. But if he wasn't an uncle, who was he? He certainly wasn't Santa Claus, not with the smell of brown ale on his breath. Or perhaps he was. Perhaps Santa Claus is everybody's uncle, and everybody's uncle is Santa Claus.

Brock's Benefit

Belated benedictions to the begetter of the Badgers Bill – the eccentric Earl of Arran.

Thanks to his kindly intervention Old Brock is now a pro-

146

tected animal and need no longer fear ending up as a shaving-brush. And a good thing too.

I have not met any badgers socially but I know people who have and they seem altogether charming fellows. (The badgers, I mean, not those who study their ways – although they too are often quite nice chaps.)

The badger is an incredibly civilised and hard-working crea-ture and fastidious with it. His sett is as neat and well laid-out as any bijou country cottage, with living room, bedroom, dining room, playroom for the cubs, and separate toilet. I wouldn't be at all surprised to hear that he has his own private study, well stocked with detective novels and back numbers of *Punch*.

Told that ants have their own police force and their own army, Dorothy Parker inquired, 'No navy, I suppose?' When I learn that the badger spring-cleans regularly and humps his bed out into the sun to be aired, I'm tempted to ask why he doesn't hire a cleaning lady from the village.

As to why this stripey-nosed carnivorous mammal should have been befriended by the House of Lords, I believe I have the answer to that. Our ruling classes owe him a tremendous debt of gratitude, for it was a badger who once defended the degenerate aristocracy against an uprising of bolshies, reds under beds and other trouble-makers, and who restored that comforting, very English status quo – a place for everyone and everyone in his place.

I am referring, of course, to the most famous Badger of all badgers, the one who saved Toad of Toad Hall from the con-sequences of his own follies in 'The Wind in the Willows'.

I don't know whether anyone else has ever spotted it, but it has always seemed to me that this golden childhood classic is a microcosm of English society as it existed before the war.

All the social groupings of that time are represented. There is Mole of the lower middle-classes – industrious, obsequious, and a great minder of his own business. There is Ratty who likes picnics and messing about in boats – put Ratty in a straw hat and blazer and you can see him eating strawberries and cream at Henley Regatta. There is Toad with his vast inherited wealth, his absurd, expensive hobbies and his lordly disdain for the common herd.

And there is Badger – sober, stolid, reliable and thoroughly decent. In real life he would be a retired colonel, a justice of the peace, the chairman of the parish council and a great writer of letters to *The Times* on the theme of fair play.

The working classes are represented either by sycophantic mice or comic policemen and obliging washerwomen – all of them harmless enough. But alas for England, there are dissidents among them.

Out in the Wild Wood lurk militant stoats and extremist weasels – a vociferous minority dedicated to bringing the country-side to its knees. When Toad, heedless of Badger's solemn warnings, pursues his career of dissipation to the point at which it lands him in jail, the stoats and weasels seize their chance and occupy Toad Hall.

It is Badger who comes to the rescue; Badger who raises a militia composed of Mole, Ratty and himself; Badger who puts down the revolution with his walloping-stick; Badger who hands Toad Hall back to its hereditary owner, for all that he is clearly unfit to run it.

We leave Toad throwing a lavish party, boasting extravagantly about the great victory, and having learned nothing from his experiences.

I once set out to prove that 'The Wind in the Willows' is a kind of Right-wing 'Animal Farm' – an elaborate parable of middle-class attitudes to the General Strike of 1926. This theory was slightly knocked on the head when I found that it was written in 1908.

Perhaps Badger has his own ideas of what it was all about. If, in the new-found safety of his orderly burrow, he has time to write an essay on the subject, he might dedicate it, in gratitude, to the Earl of Arran.

Putting Off Paradise

The Paradise Estate, built in the early nineteen-fifties on the outskirts of the city, is one of the show-places of Europe.

The gauntness of its tower blocks is softened by rolling lawns and fountains. Its cobbled piazzas are shaded by trees; its pleasant shopping centre is traffic-free.

For those who live on the Paradise Estate – mostly young

families – there is much to compensate for the bustling slum streets they have left behind.

There is a nursery school, a youth club, a community centre, a playground, a sports field, a heated swimming pool – and a good bus service back to grandma's.

There is fresh air in abundance for those who like that sort of thing, and strobe lights and juke-boxes for those who do not.

What else can I tell you about the Paradise Estate – except that it does not exist?

There is an estate of that name all right (or it may be called, depending on where it is and when work commenced, the Clem Attlee Estate or the Beveridge Estate or the Alderman Rumble-tummy Estate).

They started building it, but they never got it finished.

The tower blocks exist and people live in them. The pram sheds exist. The communal laundry exists, although it has bare brick walls instead of the tiled mural that was planned for it. The bicycle-racks exist. And that is about all.

There is no nursery school, no youth club, no community centre, no playground, no sports field, no swimming pool. The bus service is infrequent. The shopping-centre is still on the drawing-board and the fountains are lost in a rolled-up blueprint. The piazzas, instead of being cobbled, are paved with good intentions in the form of cheap tarmac, and there are steep banks of clay where the rolling lawns should be.

There must have been a slip-up somewhere.

In fact there has been a series of slip-ups and I can tell you who made them. They were made by successive Governments who got their sums wrong.

When Governments get their sums wrong, the first thing they do is to tell local councils to spend less money. When a local council has to spend less money, the first place it looks to is the Paradise Estate.

After all, youth clubs and heated swimming pools do not grow on trees and even if they did, no trees were ever planted there.

The Paradise Estate is a wreck now.

The lower reaches of the tower blocks are pocked with mud and scrawled with illiterate slogans. The doors of the pram sheds hang from their hinges. The tiniest children play on the pile of rubble where the nursery school should be; the older ones loaf around in doorways.

149

A baby was tipped out of its push-chair last week, and the week before that there was a gang fight, and the week before that some hooligans broke into the communal laundry and smashed it up.

The future of the Paradise Estate remains indefinite.

The plans for a nursery school must be 'reviewed' – that means put off. The plans for a community centre must be 'slowed down' – that means put off. The plans for other projects will be 'affected' – that means put off.

As for the trees and the rolling lawns, savings can be made by 'abating the growth in expenditure'.

That means no trees and no rolling lawns.

The directions are in a new version of Paradise Lost with the uninspiring title of 'Rate Fund Expenditure and Rate Calls in 1974–75'. Published by a Government that couldn't get its sums right.

Gurgling in their prams in the winter sunlight that filters through to the tarmac piazzas, there are infants who will see the inside of a prison cell before they are seventeen years old.

Some baffled judge will peer at them over his half-moon spectacles, completely unable to comprehend their mindless violence but determined to stamp it out. Told that there are no hostels or detention centres available, he will utter a few words of criticism against a short-sighted and parsimonious Government, and then clap them in jail as a warning to others.

Their friends on the Paradise Estate will discuss the case for half an hour, and then commence throwing stones as an alternative to doing nothing.

By that time, of course, there will be a new generation of gurgling babies out in the winter sun, facing the same future, looking up to the sky and chuckling with delight as an empty Concorde dips gracefully and heads into the flight-path down to Maplin Sands.

As Good Books Go

I was saddened to learn from a survey that two out of every three children live in homes where there are fewer than five books.

It's like hearing that two out of every three children have never tasted chocolate cake, or seen the sea, or watched Laurel and Hardy, or visited a fairground.

Reading, like cleaning one's teeth three times a day, is a habit acquired at home or nowhere. And so, although these unhappy kids may handle books at school and in the public library, most of them will grow up with no idea that they are missing one of the greatest pleasures that life has to offer.

I have touched before on the joys of discovering reading, and on the unique, never-to-be-repeated sensation of finding that the author of – say – William, which you devoured at one go, has written a whole shelf-full of stories about the same character. Serendipity, which is the art of making happy finds by chance, has an especial savour for twelve-year-old boys let loose among books.

But as well as the delight of reading books there is also the delight of owning books and this, too, as a by-product of their deprivation, is denied those two out of three children. If they were denied shoes or trousers they could be no worse off.

I was brought up not in a five-book family but in an eight-book family, so I suppose I had a better start than some. I can still see those volumes propping up the tea-caddy on the cupboard-top: the medical encyclopaedia, the gardening ditto, the two volumes of *War Illustrated,* the thick anthology of horror stories with a vampire bat embossed on the spine, the stuffy old Victorian novel entitled 'A Mountain Daisy'.

Our library was completed by the family Bible and a book about a windmill in French, which my father brought home in the hope that it would turn us all into fluent linguists. (My father's only other contribution to our cultural welfare was to buy a harp-zither on the never-never, but that saga is outside my present brief.)

From the moment I was able to read I felt keenly that we were victims of literary malnutrition, and as soon as I was old enough to earn money I began to put the deficiency right. Between the ages of eleven and eighteen I don't think I let a week go by without acquiring two or three battered volumes, usually for a few coppers. Eventually we had more books than the family next door had bed-bugs – a notable achievement.

I still have a few of those early finds, with the price scrawled in pencil on their fly-leaves: Three Men In A Boat (sixpence),

Goodbye, Mr Chips (threepence), Boswell's Life of Johnson (a shilling), a paperback W. W. Jacobs (a penny) and – a bargain at two bob – the biography of Edgar Wallace, which decided me on a life in journalism. (It was a picture of him in war correspondent's uniform that swung it: I thought, at the time, that if I could wangle my way on to the *Yorkshire Evening Post* I would get to wear a peaked cap.)

I usually bought good books as good books go, and as good books go, most of my original purchases went. They were either sold to provide me with funds to buy more, or got rid of for space reasons when I went slightly berserk and began to import sets of Dickens and other 25-volume punters.

To my everlasting regret I gave away a complete collection of green Penguin detective stories, now priceless. I bought for threepence, and also gave away, a copy of P. G. Wodehouse's first book, a heavy-handed spoof called 'Scoop, Or How Clarence Saved England'. The last time that rarity turned up in a bookseller's catalogue the asking price was £40.

As for the numerous first editions of Arnold Bennett and H. G. Wells which passed through my hands, I see they are now fetching upwards of a fiver each.

But I'm getting mercenary now, and the real value of books has nothing to do with what they're worth in money. Nor need it have much to do with what they cost in money, for you can still find incredible bargains in the few second-hand shops that haven't been pulled down to make way for 'improved amenities'.

A few weeks ago, in Bristol, I bought three modern novels, a collection of war poems, 'The Father Brown Omnibus', and a copy of 'The Army Games and Sports Manual for 1927', which I thought might make interesting reading (it didn't) – and I got away with change out of a fifty-pence piece.

I've no idea what I've spent on books in my lifetime – very much less, I would think, than I've spent on booze and tobacco: but I know which has given me the greatest lasting pleasure.

If I had to make a choice of giving toys or books to a boy of eleven or twelve I would certainly give him books. With a platoon of plastic soldiers or a model railway he has a world of his own to play with; but with a shelf or two of books he has the universe. Furthermore, books don't make a noise, and they're practically unbreakable.

Wheel Of Fortune

I found half a crown in the back of a drawer yesterday. I've been handling it ever since like a talisman.

What a thick, substantial, heavy, happy coin the half-crown was! What a fortune of a coin, what a birthday present of a coin, what a good-conduct medal of a coin!

I can remember when you were chucked off trams for proffering this milled silver cartwheel. Whoever carried change for half a dollar?

The day when there were eight of them to the pound seems as far off now as when you could have a night at the music hall, a pea and pie supper, ten Woodbines, a cab home and change out of fourpence. But it was only yesterday.

I would settle for four half-crowns to the pound, and call them 25-pence pieces if necessary if only we could have them back.

Slap-up On Sea

Whatever you may have read to the contrary in a survey published this week, a seaside resort cannot be judged by the state of its public lavatories.

No one in his right mind is going to drive sixty miles to the coast just to have a jimmy-riddle in comfort.

Nor can you judge a seaside resort by its parking, its seafront 'amenities', whatever they may be, or even its amusements, entertainments and restaurants.

You should judge a seaside resort by how vulgar it is. Solely that. Nothing else.

You may reply that some seaside resorts – Frinton-on-Sea, for example – are not vulgar. But that is flawed logic. They are not vulgar because they are not seaside resorts. They are wateringplaces. They are townships that happen to have settled, for reasons usually to do with fish or bath-chairs, at the sea's edge.

No town that puts a lawn on its sea-front (as Frinton does, and calls it a greensward at that) can be described as a seaside resort. The proper substance for a seafront is tarmac. That is why Brighton is a seaside resort and Hove is a mere sea-suburb.

The aforementioned tarmac should be fitted out with parallel metal lines and on these lines should sail strange exotic vessels, the shape of moonrockets and Mississippi steamboats, which turn out to be illuminated trams.

Any seaside resort that does not possess illuminated trams is off to a bad start. It is not vulgar enough.

It will, if it is wise, attempt to make up the discrepancy by painting all its municipal buildings bright green and flood-lighting them, by ensuring that there is a stink of fried onions from one end of the borough to the other, and by encouraging the sale of villainous-hued rock made to look like false teeth and kippers. But even these welcome exuberances will not, on their own, remove the taint of gentility.

To be really vulgar, and so qualify for the rosette, the four stars and the crossed knives and forks, a seaside resort must have (a) the biggest, tallest or longest something or other in the world, and (b) some edifice or structure that no other town has got nor, if in its right senses, would want.

Thus the seaside resort that does not boast the biggest pub in the world must boast the tallest tower or the longest pier or the fattest lady – and it must do this boasting in multi-coloured electric light bulbs.

And in addition, it must have a floral clock that plays 'Come Into The Garden, Maud' on the half-hour, or a Wurlitzer organ that can be heard in the next town, or an aquarium fashioned after the Taj Mahal, or if possible, all three.

And above and beyond and in gleeful excess of all this there must be whelks, dodgems, open-top buses, candy-floss, brown ale, jugs of sweet tea, donkeys, pleasure boats, wax museums, bingo, clock golf, brandysnap, coconut shies, Ken Dodd, pin-tables, ice-cream, human cannonballs – and souvenir thermometers so hideous, so grotesque, so malformed, that stunned friends and relatives will shrink against the wall and gibber wordlessly when presented with them.

Put these ingredients together, turn up the brilliance and the volume control, and you have got a picture of what the ideal seaside resort looks like.

What the ideal seaside resort does not even remotely look like, despite the claims of that survey I mentioned, is Bournemouth. If Bournemouth is the ideal seaside resort then I am the original Gypsy Rose Lee.

The ideal seaside resort, by my definition, is Blackpool, hotly and sweatily pursued by Southend.

Blackpool came a poor sixth in the survey, partly because some of its lavatories are not very nice and are not well signposted. Fiddlesticks.

I do not care if it directs its customers to a hole in the road and makes them wash their hands in paraffin. Blackpool, without any argument, is the most vulgar and thus the most perfect seaside town in Britain and possibly in the world, not excluding Las Vegas (which, come to think of it, does not qualify, seeing as how it is in the middle of the desert).

Blackpool is a tattooed lady of a town, a Donald McGill postcard of a town, a fish-and-six-pennorth of a town, a knees-up kiss-me-quick and chase-your-Aunt-Fanny-round-the-lighthouse of a town, a wish-you-were-here of a town.

May the fuse never blow on its Illuminations, may its Golden Mile never turn to grey, and may the draught champagne flow for ever in Yates's Wine Lodge.

Hard Graft

The Royal Commission into Backhanders, Bungs and Bunce in Local Government, which has now been sitting for fourteen years, yesterday questioned Councillor Arnold Watch-chain, formerly chairman of the Baths and Waterworks Committee of Clogthorpe District Council.

The Commission was curious to know how Clogthorpe, an obscure mining community in South Loamshire, comes to have a £200,000,000 international airport.

The Chairman asked Councillor Watch-chain if he knew a man called Slippery Sam.

Answer: Yes. He is a consultant.

Question: Does this Mr Slippery Sam sell international airports?

A: Only in his spare time. His main interest is in selling refrigerators to Eskimos. He also has a nice line in shopping precincts, conference centres, underground car parks and prestige office blocks.

Q: I believe you had several meetings with Mr Slippery Sam in the Majestic Hotel?

A: That is correct. He happened to be passing through with a business colleague, a civil engineer called Burglar Ted, and we took the opportunity to hold preliminary discussions.

Q: You yourself stayed at the Majestic Hotel, where in the course of four nights you ran up a bill for £1,629 which was paid by Mr Burglar Ted?

A: Quite right. The thing is, you see, that these talks went on far into the night and I invariably missed my last bus home.

Q: But surely, Mr Watch-chain, you live only 200 yards from the Majestic Hotel?

A: Yes, but it's uphill.

Q: And in any case, couldn't you have driven home in your Rolls-Royce Silver Cloud?

A: Normally, yes, but during the period under discussion my chauffeur had broken his arm lifting a crate of champagne out of the boot.

Q: You are a retired gas inspector, are you not, Mr Watch-chain?

A: I am.

Q: Would you mind telling us how you come to own a Rolls-Royce Silver Cloud?

A: Green Shield Stamps.

Q: At the end of your talks with Mr Slippery Sam and Mr Burglar Ted, you were convinced of Clogthorpe's need for an international airport?

A: Completely.

Q: Even though at that time, Clogthorpe was barely able to support a two-hourly bus service, and the branch line to Market Slagsbury twelve miles away had been closed down because of public apathy?

A: Slippery Sam brought it home to me very forcefully that we were not living in the nineteenth century and that Clogthorpe had to move with the times.

Q: The council's decision to build this international airport was approved in committee which at all times met behind locked doors?

A: That's right. We didn't want anyone to pinch our idea.

Q: Since you were only chairman of the Baths and Waterworks Committee, what had the airport plans got to do with you?

A: Well, you see, a feature of number 15 Arrivals Building is an Olympic-size swimming pool. There are also ornamental fountains at the end of each runway. Furthermore, we had to decide on whether to have gold taps in the men's washroom. All this came under the umbrella of the Baths and Waterworks Committee.

Q: The contract to build Clogthorpe International Airport was awarded, was it not, to Mr Slippery Sam and Mr Burglar Ted?

A: Yes. It was between them and a local builder and decorator, a Mr Pearson. We decided, after comparing tenders, that they were the best men for the job.

Q: Where was the contract signed, Mr Watch-chain?

A: Bermuda. My Auntie Nellie runs a small boarding-house there, and she had invited me to take a well-earned holiday. One day, quite by chance, I ran into Slippery Sam while out surfing. I happened to have the contract in the back pocket of my bathing trunks, so we signed it there and then with a ballpoint pen that writes under water.

Q: You returned to Bermuda a fortnight later, did you not?

A: Yes. I had forgotten my toothbrush.

Q: And you stayed in the penthouse suite of the Hotel Copacabana for a period of six months?

A: I may have done. I can't remember.

Q: Mr Watch-chain, I am bound to say that the Commission is far from satisfied with some of your replies. Would you object if we checked your statements with the Council's auditor?

A: Not at all. I'll tell him you want to see him as soon as he gets back from his round-the-world cruise.

As She Is Spoke

Corresponding with me about a recent column on the raising of the school-leaving age, several readers have asked what fifteen-year-olds who don't want to take exams may usefully be taught. I think it would be not such a bad idea if they were taught to speak English.

The other day I was stopped in the street by a youthful motorcyclist who delivered of himself the following cryptogram:

'*Norwich is a bess wire acne.*'

It made so little sense that he might have been talking in Swahili for all I knew.

'Come again?' I said.

'*Acne. Bess why.*'

Only after several of these exchanges, when he had begun to speak very slowly as if to one who was senile, did I grasp what he was saying, which was: '*Do you know which is the best way to Hackney?*'

'Yes. Straight through the lights, take the middle lane, and you'll find it signposted at the roundabout.'

'*Stray froo da lie, me lay, sigh po adder rah-bar.*'

'Correct.'

'*Tar.*'

Room Service

Many years ago, while serving King and Country (nothing fancy, you understand: I was one of those who only stand and wait), I often used the booking-hall of Euston Station as a hotel.

They did you a very commodious porter's trolley which, with a kit-bag as a pillow and a greatcoat as a blanket, was the next best thing to a fourposter.

If the porters' trolleys were booked you stretched out on a bench and if the benches were spoken for you had to pig it on the floor.

When I say 'pig it' I mean it in the most literal sense, for at three in the morning the place resembled nothing so much as a giant sty. It was, at that time, a favourite resting-post for the dregs of London. It was as if Euston Station, along with the Statue of Liberty, had put out a general call for 'your tired, your poor, your huddled masses yearning to breathe free, the wretched refuse of your teeming shore'.

In the booking-hall at Euston your huddled masses not only breathed free, they breathed stentoriously. Outside, the great Doric arch shuddered to their snoring.

It is, of course, the old Euston station I'm talking about. The new one looks more like the lobby of a bacteriological institute than a railway booking hall and loitering is not encouraged.

At night, the porters' trolleys are discreetly wheeled away.

158

There are few benches. (There were, indeed, no benches at all when this sterilised marvel was first unveiled, the argument being that they would only get cluttered up by people wanting to sit down.)

It is not a place for huddled masses. It is a place for men in white coats, hurrying silently across scrubbed marble floors on obscure technological errands.

They are great believers in technology at the new Euston. They think technology can perform wonders, such as making the trains run on time. But they are not above trying to explain their ethos to the wretched refuse of the 07.00 train to Birmingham (change at Rugby).

Currently, in the middle of that great empty, echoing vault, there is a kind of podium or stand surmounted by a surrealist winking light. A sign tells us that the purpose of this plastic caravanserai is to explain something called *MULTI-ASPECT SIGNALLING*. A series of illuminated panels tries to do just that.

I will not quote all that is written on these illuminated panels, partly because they go on at alarming length but mainly because I might just as well quote from the Rosetta Stone for all the sense it would make. But I will quote a typical passage, from a section called *AUTOMATIC TRAIN REPORTING*.

'Train running information will be fed into the general-purpose computer from the train describer and from the tele-printer network interconnecting the signal boxes and other out-stations of the Regional Control Office at Crewe.'

Crewe, Crewe! What have they done to you? I remember you when you were a sooty, sulpherous, cindery slab of type in Bradshaw. Now they've strait-jacketed you in Moon-language and Crewe could be the feeder-junction for an orbital laboratory floating about in the outer nothing. But to continue the gobbledygook:

'After processing, up-to-the-minute information will be auto-matically disseminated to wherever it is required, as well as being recorded in local signal boxes. Certain places, such as the Regional Control Office at Crewe, will be able to interrogate the computer in order to obtain classified information to meet traffic regulation requirements.'

So now you know what became of the language after Will Shakespeare had finished with it. They put it out with the empty milk bottles and it was reclaimed and recycled by a public relations man at Euston – when he had stopped his experiments on rabbits.

It is difficult to imagine who was processed to write English like that – if you want to call it English. I see him as a keen young man in a dark blue suit (he doesn't want to offend anyone) with stitch-marks round his throat where his head was sawn off and all those phrases – 'train running information', 'the train describer', 'after processing' – were poured down his gullet. Or perhaps it was all done intravenously, while he was asleep.

But I digress. The point I am coming to is that the exhibition stand where all this junk is laid out is mounted, as it just would be, on a very nice slab of blue carpet.

At three o'clock the other morning, while all was otherwise empty, dead and sterile at Euston, this slice of carpet was tightly packed with tossing, snoring, heaving, grunting vagrants, laid end-to-end like pilchards. The huddled masses had come home again.

The silly winking light that symbolises *MULTI-ASPECT SIGNALLING* blinked over them like the North Star gone mad. And the smell of meths fought the smell of antiseptic – and won.

It just shows that you *CAN* beat the system. If you completely ignore it.

Day-trip Hints

Question: I am a kind father and I have promised to give my three children a Bank Holiday treat. Can you advise me?

Answer: Yes. Never make such a damn-fool promise again, as long as you live.

Q: That is already my firm resolution. The little perishers have been bouncing up and down on my bed since 5.30 a.m., claiming that I said I would drive them to the seaside if it is a fine day.

A: Deny that you said any such thing.

Q: They have it in writing.

A: All right then – deny that it is a fine day.

Q: But the sun is streaming in through every window.

A: Tell them it is summer lightning. Tell them, furthermore, that the car has broken down.

Q: Very well, but I have got to do something to keep them out of mischief. I can hardly lock them in the linen cupboard for the day, can I?

A: Oh, I don't know so much.

Q: Be serious. Where shall I take them?

A: Tell them that if they are very good, and keep as quiet as mice, you will take them to the zoo.

Q: But Boris, my youngest, does not like the zoo.

A: That is entirely immaterial. If you are not very careful, you are going to finish up at a fun-fair, a move not to be recommended to those who have troublemakers such as young Boris in tow.

Q: I am a kind father and I have promised to take my children to the zoo. Can you give me details of bus routes?

A: Bus routes? Have you gone completely off your chump? Are you seriously proposing to expose three screaming children, one of whom does not wish to go where he is being taken, to the deficiencies of the public transport system? Take them by car.

Q: But I have already told them the car has broken down.

A: We will cross that bridge when we come to it. By the way, is that Boris, your youngest, who is making that God-awful row?

Q: Yes. He is afraid that the alligators at the zoo will eat him up.

A: I would play on that fear if I were you. Tell him that Mr Alligator is particularly partial to children who make a noise like Lucifer descending into hell when their kind father gives them a day out. Where do you think you are going?

Q: To the zoo.

A: At this hour? Don't you realise that three children, especially when one of them is clearly a tiny Trotskyite hell-bent on causing bother, can suck a zoo dry in forty-five minutes flat? They will be bored stiff by noon and whining to go to a fun-fair. Tell them you have to go out first.

Q: Where shall I tell them I am going?

A: To see a man about having the car mended. I told you I'd get you off that particular hook, didn't I?

Q: I am a kind father who has lied to his children and is now out of the house. Where do I go now?

A: Round this corner.

Q: I have now gone round this corner and find myself opposite a public house called the Goat and Boots. What is my next step?

A: Enter it. And incidentally, it's your round.

Q: It is now three o'clock, and I have wasted most of the day buying drinks for a man who claims to be the greatest living expert on how to give my children a Bank Holiday treat. Isn't it time I took them to the zoo?

A: Wouldn't they prefer to play ludo quietly among themselves?

Q: No.

A: I only ask, because I happen to know a rather good afternoon drinking club but a short step from here. Do your children, including the subversive Boris, realise that it is coming on to rain?

Q: No it isn't. They may be small but they are not raving idiots. It is clearly and obviously a delightful afternoon.

A: Off you go, then, but don't say I didn't warn you.

Q: About what?

A: You'll see.

Q: I am a kind father who has been conned and smooth-talked into taking his three children to the zoo. I cannot describe to you the experience I have had, especially with Boris, my youngest. Now it is five o'clock and they are all lost. What do you advise?

A: Ask around. Try the alligator house first.

Breaking The Mould

Contrary to the belief of many high-ups in the Labour Party, most people in this country do not resent belonging to the Common Market. But they do resent belonging to Europe.

The distinction, which I am about to explain, is not a particularly subtle one. But it fuzzes up the question of our future in the Market to the point where any popular answer must become valueless.

When the dreaded referendum comes, my guess is that the antis among us will be voting not against the agricultural policy nor even against the Brussels junta who are suspected (quite wrongly) of plotting to abolish the King Edward potato.

They will be voting against juggernauts, VAT, decimalisation, standardisation, centralisation, carbonated beer, lavatory doors in three languages, cryptic foreign road-signs, the STD telephone, the Centigrade thermometer, the 24-hour clock – and the ten-to-the-dozen bunch of tulips.

All of which are as European as croissants for breakfast. But we would be putting up with them by now whether we'd signed on the dotted line or not.

Some time after the war, those important men who brood upon our future had a remarkable vision. They saw a new, vital, get-up-and-go, export-or-die Great Britain that was to corner world trade while Japan was still struggling to put together its first transistor radio.

They saw a land criss-crossed with motorways, every motorway leading to a port, and every port jam-packed with refrigerated containers.

They saw international airports in the unlikeliest corners of Essex and Lancashire. They saw hypermarkets and multi-storey car parks. They saw high-rise hives where the worker bees of the assembly line could rest between shifts. They saw miles of conveyor belts piled with every consumer item known to man – in brightly-coloured plastic.

They were out to sweep the cobwebs away, these people. They were impatient of our silly little English ways – our fussy currency, our rods, poles and perches, our corner shops with the cat asleep on the bacon slicer. They wanted change, and they got it.

And all this began to happen when the Common Market was but a steely glint in General de Gaulle's eye.

Now of course this weather-beaten old country of ours had to be modernised. You cannot flood the world with panti-hose and Union Jack matchbox-covers unless you have electricity and main drainage. But the wise men who planned it got it all wrong.

They thought they were Europeanising Britain. 'Getting into line with Europe,' they called it. But they knew as much about the real Europe outside the Fiat plant gates as I know about playing the saxophone.

In the last couple of years I've spent several weeks trotting round the various Common Market countries – not just the capitals but the smallish towns where ordinary life goes on.

The first thing you notice about these places is that they are not pulling them down. Although as bang-up-to-date as most English cities – and more up-to-date than many – they retain their character, even their eccentricity.

Bruges, unlike Burnley, does not boast of having created 'an entirely new shopping world where the time-worn 100-year-old market hall stood amid cobbled humdrum streets'. Europe retains its cobbles, and they are not so humdrum.

The other thing you notice is that no one is in a blind panic to keep up with the country next door. You do not hear businessmen in Denmark talking about 'getting into line' with Western Germany. Amsterdam does not try to look like Brussels. These different Europeans have pride, and, what is more important, faith, in their individual ways of life.

If we have lost that kind of faith, it is because it was taken away from us by those important men of vision. Although they had such confidence in Britain, they had none at all in the British. We had to be 'brought into line' – or no one would believe we were serious about joining the modern world.

The result, of course, is that Britain has become the most European country in Europe – but only in the sense that it now seems like a foreign land to the people who live here.

This process of moulding Britain to a completely non-existent standard continues – and we've had just about enough of it. Although no one talks about it much, there is a deep, widespread, very English desire not to be mucked about any more – to be left alone, to be done with chopping and changing.

Our great fear, a mistaken one, is that the further we get into Europe the more this mucking-about process must continue – that there is no way of stopping it. The referendum may produce the result that Mr Wilson expects. But many will be answering a question that hasn't been asked.

The Big Store

Pulling Gamages down presents one big problem for the demolition men – how are they going to get the customers out of the joint?

One of the many endearing features of this rambling, eccentric bazaar is that once inside its labyrinthine halls it is almost impossible to find your way back to the street.

Built somewhat on the Chinese box principle the house of Gamage lures you ever-further into its bewildering interior – up ramps and down little flights of stairs, through archways and over internal foot-bridges, round corners, across endless mezzanines and half-landings.

I swear that you can go upstairs from the second floor and somehow find yourself in the basement.

There are various illuminated arrows and direction signs but seasoned explorers in the jungle of Holborn know that these are meant only to add to the confusion. Often is the time when I have popped into Gamages for a birthday card, found myself stranded in the food hall or the sports department, and staggered out via the fire exit clutching a bag of self-raising flour or a tennis racquet.

This Hampton Court Maze among department stores is to be replaced, need I say, by the usual office block. The mournful reason given for its demise is that Gamages has not kept up with the times. Often I think it would be a nicer world had time stopped still with Gamages.

Play It Again, Sam

I was reading that the television companies expect to be in something of a quandary when it comes to showing old movies in a few years' time. This year's brew, it seems, may have a little too much body for the family audience.

I can see the problem. On ITV the other night the announcer gave this chirpy summary of the kind of slightly-used film currently available: 'Sharks, buried treasure and Yvonne de Carlo's legs – what more do you want?'

What we want, apparently – or more accurately, what Wardour Street thinks we want – is rape, incest, transvestism, full-frontal nudity, lesbianism and necrophilia.

Not even Mrs Whitehouse would claim, television-wise, that we can get all that at home.

'Bedroom Mazurka', 'Whithout a Stitch', 'Girls for Pleasure' and 'I had My Brother's Wife' are among the potential old movies now showing in the West End. I can't see any of them occupying the Saturday afternoon slot on BBC–2.

One way out of the dilemma would be simply to show the vintage collection already in hand over and over again.

But let's explore another possible solution, which is that when TV runs out of old movies it could start showing old television.

We're getting that to some extent already, of course. But I'm not talking about another chance to make sense out of one of last year's Wednesday plays – I'm talking about really *old* TV, the cathode-ray equivalent of 'Broadway Melody of 1938'.

How many people would like to see a re-run of 'The Grove Family', for example? Or 'The Quatermass Experiment'?

I can remember nothing of the former series except an old grandmother perpetually eating boiled sweets, and nothing of the latter except that one of the leading players was a heap of sludge. From this distance the two characters seem interchangeable. But there was a time when both programmes were compulsive weekly viewing in millions of darkened rooms. Could they ever be compulsive viewing again?

I expect the BBC would argue that the world has moved on a bit since those days and that they have to cater for a more sophisticated audience. But if we've grown out of 'The Apple-yards' why aren't we supposed to have grown out of all those Mickey Rooney college musicals, or those scores of Westerns where the drunken Doc calls for hot water and lots of it?

A more forceful argument would be that most of this stuff went out live and no trace of Granny Grove and/or the Sludge Monster remains. Even so, there are hundreds of old programmes that do still exist, and it's worth asking why the TV companies don't bother to show them.

Do you remember all those detectives who were never off the screen in the early days of ITV? They were always getting in and out of sports cars in the vicinity of Big Ben, they all spoke in mid-Atlantic accents, and English expressions were always translated into American – 'There was a quarter of a million

166

pounds in that safe, Carstairs – that's nearly seven hundred thousand dollars.'

Each instalment ended with detective and criminal grappling on the floor with pauses for explanatory dialogue – 'There's just one thing I don't understand, Inspector...' 'Quite simple, Carstairs. You made just one little mistake...'

It was a rare week indeed when the villain wasn't tracked down by means of a carelessly-dropped bookmatch containing the name, address and telephone number of his Soho club.

This was inspired hokum on a scale that even Hollywood at its dottiest would have found it hard to approach. And yet, when the TV companies strive to satisfy the undoubted market for time-honoured baloney, they always plump for the imported rather than the home-cured variety.

It cannot be that those early TV series were all that badly made, for some of the 'B' pictures currently slinking on to the small screen were even more badly made. The only other explanation is that old television totally lacks the nostalgic appeal of old movies or even of old radio.

It was still possible recently to find a sizeable audience for 'The Goon Show', and even the worst old pre-war British film – and they don't come any worse than that – will find a ready market.

There will be no revival of 'The Grove Family', not because it was primitive television but because the demand simply isn't there.

TV is too much of the moment to leave any magic trail behind it. Compulsive it may be – memorable it is not. Who were the stars of 'Destination – Downing Street', which was ITV's first serial?

So it looks as if my first solution to TV's problem was the right one. Just keep right on with those old Humphrey Bogarts.

Play it again, Sam.

End Of The Rainbow

There must be a cheaper way of contemplating that the end of the world is nigh. Here I am in the South of France, basking under the palm trees and musing on over-population, stress, pollution and all the other ills that the earth is heir to. No wonder I don't get a suntan.

The Riviera used to be called the playground of the rich. It still is – but there are more of them about. Not only do the rich get richer, they multiply like Angora rabbits.

I've paid fifteen bob for the privilege of lying on some stones. Space on what is humorously called the beach is in such demand that the territory marked out for me is no bigger than a coffin.

If I stretch out my right arm, it touches an American family who've come 3,000 miles to toss Coca-Cola cans into the sea. If I waggle my left foot it comes into contact with a Scandinavian couple who've travelled across Europe to listen to their transistor radio.

The blue Mediterranean bobs with wine bottles, lettuce leaves and patches of diesel oil. Out in the bay, a moored submarine guards our way of life with all the reassuring aplomb of a tethered shark.

The balmy air is hideous with the sound of hovercraft, jets coming in to land, motor boats, piped music, light aircraft touting advertising banners, car horns and the steady whine of Frenchmen demanding tips in four languages.

This jam-packed, shrieking corner of Paradise is an expensive preview of what life has in store for all of us – too many people making too much muck and too much noise with too little space to do it in.

I reflect that it's all part of the price of affluence and I decide to relax and skim through a magazine. The first thing I read is that all known deposits of gold, silver, platinum, tin, zinc, lead, natural gas and helium will be exhausted within the next twenty years.

Then I arrive at one of the most chilling sentences I have ever seen: *Mines Bear No Second Crop.* When the last nugget has been dug, that's it. There'll be nothing left but a hole in the ground.

The sunbathers go on sunbathing and the American family throw another tin can into the sea. Never mind, there's plenty more where that came from. But not for long, baby, not for long.

On the Riviera, you could once make-believe that the world was a very rich place to live in. Now, even through the rose-coloured spectacles of the Côte d'Azur, the world is beginning to look like what it is – overcrowded, dirty, noisy, smelly, and rapidly running out of resources. We're nearing the end of the rainbow, with not a crock of gold in sight.

Apart from that – wish you were here.

Keep Off The Grass

A neighbour of mine has just turned in his London flat and gone to live in the suburbs. The move has cost him £1,500 in cash, an extra twelve pounds a month in mortgage payments, thirty shillings a week in train fares and two hours a day in travelling time.

For this he gets four extra rooms that he doesn't need, a garage for a car he can't afford, some stone gnomes, and about four hundred square yards of what botanists call *Festuca Duriuscula* and the rest of us call grass.

Of course it was the grass, and only the grass, that persuaded him to reorganise his life as drastically as if he had gone into a monastery or joined the army. He talks smugly about investing in bricks and mortar but he knows, and everybody else knows, that he has invested in grass.

Like every Englishman, he grew up with rich obsessional fantasies about this stuff. He imagines himself lying out on it, sunbathing. Or stretched over it in a hammock, listening to the Test scores. Or gently mowing it on a Sunday morning. He doesn't realise, yet, that for 315 days out of the year it will be sopping wet, that you have only to go indoors for a deckchair and it becomes choked with weeds or that it will probably give you hayfever.

I once owned some grass myself – bequeathed to me by a previous tenant who had gone to pastures newer and bigger. I had no particular use for it so I thought I'd cover it up with paving stones and make a patio.

But grass, among its many other faults, can't take a hint. When summer came it began to force its way up through the cracks, and there was nothing for it but to lie in wait with a pair of nail-scissors, decapitating each blade as it cropped up. After a time, I retired with backache and the grass, flushed with success, joined forces with some kind of mossy substance and began to make inroads across the whole patio. Soon you couldn't walk three steps out of the house without skidding on to your backside. So I moved.

My dislike for grass goes back to my childhood. I grew up surrounded by it. This was on a municipal housing estate which was a very good place if you were a goat but not exciting for the five or six thousand families who had to live there. There was no pub, no cinema, no public library, church, playground, bowling green, tennis court, coffee bar, youth club or bingo hall – not even a park bench. But there was grass.

The stuff was there by the acre, wherever you looked, in every kind of shape – in squares and ovals, diamonds and triangles, half-moons, crescents and ellipses. If they could have found a way of arranging it in cubes they would have done so.

The centre of the estate was marked by a vast circular lawn big enough to take the Olympic Games. But you couldn't play on it, you couldn't sit on it, you couldn't even walk across it. It was to look at. On Sundays the citizens of this place used to do just that. They would come out of their houses, walk up to the wire fence surrounding this green, treeless moonscape, stare blankly for a while and then go home again. There was nothing else to do.

Eventually a mob of kids tore up the railings, trampled on the grass, and made a new sport of throwing clumps of earth at passing old-age pensioners. The estate got a reputation for vandalism and the council made constructive efforts to get at the root of the trouble. They put new fences around the grass. Higher ones.

The place I've described happens to be in Yorkshire but I could take you to a hundred others, in a dozen other counties, that are exactly like it.

I have taken some trouble to find out who is to blame for this state of affairs. The culprit was a man named Ebenezer Howard, the pioneer of garden cities. This Ebenezer Howard had a number of ideas about rehousing the slums, ranging from the visionary to the crackpot. Among them was what he called 'the marriage of town and country', by which he meant that people in cities should have their fair whack of trees, streams, meadows, cows and other rural delights. With this idea firmly in his head Ebenezer came up with an important formula which became the magic nostrum of town and country planning: no more than twelve houses to the acre.

This formula has been blindly and uncritically followed by local councils for half a century. It still is, except in places where not unnaturally they've suddenly run out of land and have had to start stuffing everybody into fourteen-storey blocks of flats.

Elsewhere it's almost an established practice, almost a constitutional right, that when you're plucked out of a slum terrace and put in one of these council-house ghettos, you're entitled to one back garden, one front garden, one sapling, and a view of the communal lawn. They may have pulled down the corner shop, the fleapit cinema, the pub, the newspaper kiosk and all the other oddball things that made a city worth living in. You may be bored and depressed, you may have to wait an hour for the bus to work and tramp two miles to the nearest supermarket, but by God you can grow your own carrots.

Some town-planners are beginning to realise, at last, that people go quietly berserk in these places. So they build, in harmony with the rolling lawns, a structure of glass and pine and ping-pong tables called a community centre – the civic equivalent of a heart transplant. Anxiously, they feel the corporate pulse of the marooned population. Hopefully, they announce that the patient is rallying and is able to play a little bingo.

I wonder what would happen if by some happy freak of nature it wasn't possible to cultivate grass under urban conditions. Supposing it just had to remain where it belongs, in the fields and meadows – the divorce, on grounds of incompatibility, of town and country. How would the planners fill up all those squares and circles and diamonds that look so very neat on their drawing-boards? With coloured pebbles, knowing their imaginations.

Still, some day it might conceivably begin to dawn on them, when they've got their heads out of the barrel of lawn-seed, that a new community doesn't necessarily have to look nice, it has to look lived-in.

Dwight Eisenhower, when he was president of Columbia University, once received complaints that students were damaging the campus lawns by taking short cuts across them. This was his solution: 'Why not build paths where the students want to walk?' I always liked Ike after that.

Ask A Silly Question

With tables of percentages dancing before my eyes, I gave up trying to make sense of the latest batch of public opinion polls and fell to day-dreaming about the private life of the gent who thinks up the questions.

I imagine him as a precise sort of cove with thin lips, rimless spectacles, polished shoes and a row of ballpoint pens in his top pocket. His name, I fancy, is Esmond. He won many scholarships.

He lives with his mother in a neat little semi which is the suburban meridian between the territorial longitudes of office and municipal tennis court. He rises at 7.30. Asked whether he would prefer a breakfast of boiled egg, fried egg, poached egg or scrambled egg, he replies that he does not know.

At 8.19 exactly, after a cup of black coffee, he folds up his newspaper, picks up his briefcase and taps the barometer.

'Mother, do you think that it is going to be an extremely sunny day for the time of year, a moderately sunny day for the time of year, a fairly sunny day with intermittent showers, or not a sunny day at all!'

'I should take your raincoat, dear,' replies his mother.

Esmond arrives at the office at nine and toils quietly at his interminable questionnaires until it is time for his lunchtime sandwiches. He is an efficient worker and only once does he need to seek advice from his superior.

'Pardon me sir, but would you say my question about the Common Market referendum is extremely long-winded, moderately long-winded, not long-winded at all, or that you have no idea what I am talking about?'

'It'll do,' says the boss shortly. 'Chuck it in with the others.' He does not like Esmond, who he believes to be after his job. The boss belongs to the old school of public opinion polls where you took a straight yes, no or don't know for an answer.

With the aid of an English grammar, Esmond spends his afternoon framing a tortuous question about whether the popularity of Harold Wilson as Prime Minister would have been higher, lower, or just about the same had he still been in office on February 29, 1972.

At 5.30 he straightens his blotter, puts his mackintosh over his arm, switches off all the office lights and repairs to the pub across the street.

'Evening Esmond,' says the barmaid.

'Good evening to you. Are you keeping well, fairly well, not very well, very unwell, or don't you know whether you are feeling well or not?'

'Mustn't grumble, Esmond. Usual?'

Esmond joins a group of regulars who are discussing ladies' bottoms and the going at Aintree. Everyone drinks up, and it is Esmond's shout.

'If I were to offer to get the next round, would your response be one of amazement, not much amazement, astonishment, not much astonishment, surprise, not much surprise, interest, not much . . .'

But by this time someone has got fed up and ordered them in.

'Cheers, Esmond.'

'Down the hatch, one and all. Is it your opinion that this beer is (a) off, (b) not really off but not at its best, (c) not off at all, or (d) that you are drinking gin and tonic?'

There is a lull in the conversation. The discussion on ladies' bottoms and the Grand National has foundered somewhat. Esmond tries to enliven the mood.

'Do you think this pub is better than the Goat in Boots, worse than the Goat in Boots, no better and no worse than the Goat in Boots, better than the Goat in Boots was this time last year but not better than the Goat in Boots is now, worse than the Goat in Boots is now but better than . . .'

Esmond suddenly notices that the pub is entirely empty. He thinks about going home for a cup of hot chocolate and a browse through the Annual Abstract of Statistics.

But he is feeling lonely. He has been feeling lonely ever since Miss Simms of Random Samples turned down his proposal of marriage. ('If I were to ask you to become my wife, would your reaction be very enthusiastic, quite enthusiastic, not enthusiastic, fairly unenthusiastic . . . ?')

Over a Cornish pasty and a shandy, Esmond wonders whether it would be a good idea to drop in on the tennis club dance, or quite a good idea to drop in on the tennis club dance, or not a good idea to drop in on the . . .

He gets there in the end because he has nowhere else to go. He is cheered up by the lights and the music and there is this pristine-looking girl in the white dress sitting all by herself. She smiles When he asks her to dance and there is an exciting whiff of perfume when they take the floor. Her head is on his shoulder.

'Tell me,' says Esmond in a husky voice, 'do you come here often, fairly often, not very often, very rarely, only on special occasions, hardly ever . . . ?'

Past Imperfect

I don't know whether you're familiar with the Sailors' Home in Liverpool – the only building I have ever come across that is fashioned after the inside of a ship.

It's an incredible Victorian extravagance of cast-iron galleries, carved wooden cabins and heroic statues – a cross between St Pancras and the SS Titanic.

The Sailors' Home is a unique landmark and so naturally they're about to pull it down to make way for an office block.

If it had been a hundred years older and Lord Nelson had once spent the night there, then no doubt this crenellated folly would have become a national monument and no one would dare lay a finger on it.

It always seemed a pity to me that we tend to preserve only the snootier type of old building – the castles, the cathedrals, the palaces, the stately homes.

Quite right that we should, of course. Our heritage, and all that sort of thing. Pay your two-bob at the turnstile and please do not touch the exhibits.

But the ordinary people, too, had their history and nowhere is it better reflected than in the sooty architecture of our industrial cities. The cloth halls and the corn exchanges, the mills and the railway viaducts, the eccentric factories built to resemble Moorish knocking-shops, even the grim Victorian workhouses – they tell us as much about the country we live in as, for example, does Windsor Castle. And slowly they're disappearing.

It is a sad and somewhat eerie experience to return to your home town only to discover that all evidence of your once having lived there has been removed by the bulldozer.

Perhaps the chapel on the corner wasn't quite up to Inigo Jones standards, and you would never have mistaken the statue of Alderman Rumbletummy for the Venus de Milo. And, of course, the slums have got to come down, for where else could they build the motorway?

But does it all have to go? Do we really want to kid ourselves that, architecturally speaking, the Industrial Revolution never happened? And will some future John Betjeman conclude that nothing of note took place in English history between the Battle of Blenheim and the completion of the M4?

Home From Home

When I was sixteen I was employed, for a short time, as resident poet to a firm of estate agents.

My job was to look at derelict slum cottages with the eye of a Keats or Shelley and transform them, in a few well-chosen words, into desirable bijou residences.

Thus a ratty backyard would become a patio, a couple of sooty apple-trees in the shade of the railway embankment would blossom forth as a walled orchard, and some dank, malodorous cellar, suitable only for bricking-up the victims of the local Bluebeard, would rise on wings of song to the status of half-basement.

My free verse appeared in selected journals under the heading, 'Properties for Sale'.

I was reminded of this early excursion into the world of letters by the recent experience of a friend of mine.

Having lived frugally for a number of years in an ordinary sort of semi in an ordinary sort of suburb, he thought it was high time to start edging himself up the accommodation ladder.

He went to the estate agents and asked them to sell his house and find him a better one. Nothing too grand, mark you – just so long as it had a bit more room and a bigger garden, and if humanly possible could it be less than three miles from the buses and the shops.

A few weeks later he got a circular offering him the next best thing to Blenheim Palace.

It was a charming modern residence in mellow red brick, situated in a much sought-after backwater and yet surrounded by shops, bus-stops, parks, schools and every possible amenity.

This Ideal Home was in immaculate condition throughout. Each window was a sun-trap, each spacious room a dazzle of light and warmth. The rose-gardens, lawns, herbaceous borders and various covered walks were all well-kept.

The price was right.

On the off-chance that such a paradise of bricks and mortar had not been snapped up already, my friend rang the agents and asked if he could view it at once.

There was a dry snigger at the other end of the telephone. The estate agent's clerk had a sense of humour.

'You can view the house any time you like,' he said, 'seeing as how you're living in it.'

How To Suck Eggs

I wonder if old people ever get fed up of being talked about as if they were all completely ga-ga.

It is one thing for us to be properly concerned about their welfare. It is quite another to treat them like a pack of infants. Because they have earned their pensions it doesn't follow that they have to be patronised, or that they particularly relish a pat on the head from their juniors.

Government Ministers are among the worst offenders. There is an unctuousness about their pronouncements on the old which, if I were of pensionable age, I think I would find downright offensive.

This sickly, condescending approach continues down the line. 'Old people must be kept at a constant temperature,' says a well-meaning notice outside my local town hall. Quite right to warn them of the dangers of hypothermia – but do we have to make them sound like so many pet rabbits?

The gas crisis is another example. All the official warnings seem to assume that no one over sixty-five can tell one end of a gas-tap from the other. Again, it's better to be safe than sorry – but it's worth pointing out that most old-age pensioners were handling gas appliances of the most hair-raising complexity long before the rest of us could reach an electric light switch.

None of this is to suggest, of course, that we shouldn't keep a constant eye on our older neighbours, who may well be given to falling downstairs or leaving their purse behind in the grocer's. But absent-mindedness and stiffening of the joints are not necessarily signs of rheumatism of the brain.

Yes, Virginia, There Is A Scrooge

Many years ago a little girl called Virginia wrote to an American newspaper to ask if it was the truth that there was a Santa Claus.

The editor's reply has become a classic. 'He exists as certainly as love and generosity and devotion exist,' wrote this good and simple man. 'Yes, Virginia, there is a Santa Claus.'

Well now, assuming that Virginia has not lost her sense of curiosity over the years, she may by this time, having grown up and seen a little of the world, be wondering about another well-known Christmas character. Is there really, Virginia might ask, any such person as Scrooge?

This time it falls on me to give the answer.

Is there a Scrooge?

Virginia, you might as well ask if there is bad luck, or bad temper, or bad manners, or whether there is any such condition as a fit of melancholy on rainy mornings.

You cannot touch these things, Virginia, but you would not deny that they exist. And so does Scrooge.

What does it matter that no one has ever seen him? Have you ever seen the malevolent spirit who makes you miss the last bus or ladders your tights or causes the bread to fall jam-side downwards?

Of course you haven't, Virginia. But that's no proof that these things don't happen, for you know they do.

Virginia, if there is no Scrooge, who do you think is responsible for all the pettiness and callousness and lack of imagination that you find in the world? You're not to blame, and your friends aren't to blame, so who is?

When an old lady's pension is cut on a technicality, when the homeless are turned away, when the children's swings are chained up, when this or that event is banned in the public interest, when pets are forbidden and the kissing has to stop, there, Virginia, if you look hard enough, you will always find Scrooge.

Or there you would find him, I should have said, if he were not hiding behind the coat-tails of officialdom. And officialdom will always swear that he hasn't been seen today, or that he went the other way.

They will tell you, when you point out Scrooge's unmistakeable handiwork, that this was an isolated case or that it was the computer's fault or that there has been an administrative error, or that rules are rules.

Don't believe them, Virginia. A person of flesh and blood works the computer, and makes the rules and then enforces them, and that person is Scrooge.

Scrooge thrives on rules, Virginia. He believes in them, far more than you believe in him. And he believes in order, duty, and the small print in the contract. What he does not believe in is creating precedents, for when you create precedents it means that if one person has been made happy then everyone else might want to be happy likewise.

Virginia, this is a world of opposites. The opposite of joy is misery and the opposite of generosity is meanness and the opposite of charity is spite. But these things are intangibles and they can only be brought to life as parasitic growths in a human shell where love, kindness, humour and tolerance have long departed.

When an old-age pensioner is worried out of her mind, it is because some person is creating that worry. When a child is disappointed, it is because some person has caused that disappointment. When the music stops abruptly, it is not usually because the orchestra has run out of breath.

Not believe in Scrooge? You may as well not believe in January.

If there were no Scrooge, Virginia, there would be carolsinging all year long. Theatres would open on Sunday. Pubs would close at one in the morning, or when they pleased. There would be café tables on the pavement, and dancing without a licence, and no such thing as the law of obstruction. Post office clerks would smile.

But as long as the people's spirit can be quenched, and laughter can be stopped, and a regulation can be found to prevent innocent enjoyment or even ordinary peace of mind, then Scrooge will flourish.

He exists all right, Virginia. He exists as certainly as red tape and petty-mindedness and over-zealousness and pusillanimity exist.

Yes, Virginia, there is a Scrooge.

No Jam Tomorrow

Twenty-seven years ago my friend Ginger and I walked out of the Youth Employment Bureau and sallied forth to revolutionise the means of production, distribution and exchange.

I was going to revolutionise the funeral business and he was going to revolutionise the jam, marmalade, lemon-curd and mincemeat game.

We were enthusiastic members of a way-out, not to say loony, socialist splinter-group dedicated to the proposition that workers should control the factories and share in their profits.

Much the same idea has recently occurred to some of the Upper Clyde shipworkers. We were ahead of our time.

'What progress have you made in the undertaking lark?' asked Ginger when we called our two cadres together a week later.

'Little,' I reported. 'In fact none. Embalmers and pallbearers, by the nature of their employment, are conservative beings. Talk to them about the need for equality and they reply that all men are equal when they are six feet under.

'How are you getting on in the jam, marmalade, lemon-curd and mincemeat racket?'

'Badly,' replied Ginger. 'The trouble with those people is that they are all well-paid, contented and thoroughly pleased with the way things are already. Indeed, they sing at their work.

'You cannot make revolutionaries,' he said, 'out of people who sing while they are making strawberry jam.'

Shortly after that gloomy conference we became interested in girls, and socialism took a back seat for a while.

The years rolled on.

Today, the funeral parlour where I served my political apprenticeship still thrives, but the jam factory where my missionary friend served his is about to close down.

It is not that it has started making inferior jam, sub-standard marmalade, imperfect lemon-curd or indifferent mincemeat. Its products remain excellent.

So – despite the attentions of Ginger twenty-seven years ago – do its labour relations. There has never been a strike in the firm's history. As Ginger had bitter reason to note, its staff of 590 boast that they were a contented and happy workforce.

They will shortly be drawing the dole for no other reason than that, in some obscure financial transaction, the factory was taken over by one of those giant food combines. And now, of course, it is to be 'rationalised' out of existence.

The prospect of unemployment takes different people in different ways.

In a letter to the Daily Telegraph, the Earl of Rosslyn begged leave to contend that the figure of nearly 1,000,000 out of work was a distorted and inaccurate one. Among his reasons was the suggestion that 'there is a hard core of people who do not want to work under any circumstances'.

A few days earlier, a hard core of once-contented, unrevolutionary jam-workers had inserted this dignified and poignant announcement in the small-ads column of the Yorkshire Evening Post:

'For hire. A compact force of male and female workers offer their services to any industrialist.'

So far there have been no takers.

Perhaps, 27 years ago, young Ginger and I should have tried harder.

Last Words

A somewhat bohemian character of my acquaintance was plucked out of his garret in deepest Soho and hurried to the suburban bedside of his father, who was gravely ill.

As he tiptoed into the sick-room the old man opened his eyes, beckoned his son closer, and uttered these immortal last words:

'When are you going to get your bleeding hair cut?'

Then he sank back into the pillows and quietly expired. It was, my friend reports, a most moving farewell.

Mad Hatter's Castle

I have always admired architects for their professional dedication. Their ideas are so consistently barmy that there must be a strict code of daftness or solemn crackpot oath which is framed in gold in every drawing office.

Glorious inconsistence is the cornerstone of this planned lunacy.

Over the years architects have believed that houses should be spaced out, that they should be crammed together, that people should live near their work, that they should live apart from their work, that tower blocks are the answer to modern living, that tower blocks are not the answer to modern living, that cities should be built on rafts floating about the Atlantic, and that large holes should be scooped out of the earth wherein we will all live like moles.

Their contradictory monuments to folly co-exist in a patchwork environment which is itself a sodium-illuminated testimonial to architectural ineptitude.

Going back to the old drawing-board once more, the bricks-and-mortar boffins have now suggested (to the public inquiry into London's development plan) that we should live in one another's gardens.

It is the thesis of a large group of architects that the city's housing problem may be partly solved by building extra houses in the commodious suburban gardens which their predecessors made the great mistake of planning in bygone years.

A generation hence, of course, future architects will declare that this notion too was all a ghastly mistake, and that the only place to build new houses is on the roofs of old ones, or in the middle of Epping Forest, or down the main sewer.

I Remember It Well

As one who has made a cottage industry of childhood reminiscence and resents all competition, I have been quietly smirking to myself over the discomfiture of my friend Harry.

Harry is my closest rival in remembrance of things past. For every street game, skipping rhyme or playground ballad I can dredge up out of my subsconscious, Harry can dredge up half a dozen.

He knows the full authorised version of 'Hark the herald angels sing, Mrs Simpson's got the King', where I can only struggle through the first two lines.

He can still speak back-slang fluently.

The man is insufferable.

Harry comes from Blackburn in Lancashire and having married recently he decided to dragoon his wife into a nostalgic trip to the old home town.

They took the M6 and turned off into the Memory Lane slip-road in the vicinity of Wigan.

At the first whiff of a cotton mill it all came flooding back for Harry – the clogs and the black puddings and the brass bands and the time he fell in the canal.

He must have bored his wife rigid.

Soon they were on the outskirts of Blackburn, and Harry began to recognise the landmarks of his childhood – the recreation ground where he used to play, the sooty old church where he'd been a choirboy, the corrugated-iron scout hut where he learned the Law and Promise of the Wolf Cubs (which he can still recite in full).

Cruising up and down the cobbled streets, Harry shed a tear for the corner sweetshop that had vanished, and another for the old-fashioned butcher's that was now a supermarket.

He held a short requiem for the hole in the ground where the pawnshop had been.

He located his old infants' school and several well-remembered pubs and the very kerbstone where he'd once tripped up and grazed his knee.

Harry was in the middle of a prolonged search for the steam laundry where his mother used to work when Mrs Harry, somewhat tartly, reminded him that it was dinner-time.

They drove on into the centre of Blackburn, following the old tram route that he knew so well, and began to look for their hotel.

They had been looking for it for half an hour when it slowly began to dawn on Harry that they were not in Blackburn at all but in Bolton, thirteen miles away.

The Postman's Trousers

For several months I've had on my desk a yellowing newspaper cutting reporting a question that was asked in the House of Commons about the number of postmen bitten by dogs. The figures given by the Postmaster General were 2,942 in 1966, 3,046 in 1967 and 3,183 in 1968.

The reason I'm reluctant to throw this item away is that, like the Dead Sea Scrolls, it seems to contain some elusive information that is tantalisingly *there* if I only knew how to look for it.

Does it mean that more postmen are being bitten by more dogs? Or that more postmen are being bitten by the same number of dogs?

Or that the same number of postmen are being bitten by the same number of dogs, but more often?

I don't have a head for statistics. They bewilder and worry me. I don't believe half of them, and I don't understand the other half. What I'm sure of, now that I've forced myself to think about them, is that they're breeding like rabbits.

Some time ago I read that by the late 1980s there will be twice as many cars on the road. I was still trying to assimilate this when I read a few weeks later that by the late 1980s there will be twice as many coloured people in Britain.

Now do all these statisticians work with each other, or do they reach their conclusions separately? The man working out the car statistics, for instance – did he have that information about the coloured population, or was he assuming that the coloured population would remain the same? Because it seems to me that his figures are wildly out. The coloured population, as it exists now, will like everyone else have twice as many cars by the late 1980s – but if it is going to double in size, surely it will have four times as many cars?

And this brings us to coloured postmen who drive cars. Obviously, within twenty years, four times as many of them will be getting bitten by dogs. But we still haven't allowed for the annual rise in the PMG's figures, which seem to indicate that the postman/dogbite rate is going up by 4 per cent a year. This means that by the end of the 1980s the figure will have nearly doubled on those for 1966, so that *eight times* more coloured postmen who drive cars will be getting bitten by dogs.

Some years ago a bank in California made a survey of its business and solemnly announced that by the end of 1970, on present trends, it would have to employ the entire population of California as clerks to get through the growing volume of work.

To the ordinary man, a statement like that is the most arrant bloody nonsense, on the level of my predictions about postmen. Certainly, I would imagine that the Californian bank was getting bogged down by paperwork, and its first job should have been to look at the vast amount of useless bumph that was being passed from one desk to another and do something about cutting it down.

But that isn't the way the office mind works – not since the computer was invented. For of course the whole purpose of that mind-boggling announcement was to soften up the bank's customers for the arrival of computer methods.

We all know what's happened since. The computer system has spread from banks to every other kind of public service, and it's a lucky man indeed who doesn't get an electricity bill for two million pounds at least once.

Let's get back to the postmen for a minute. Putting aside the intriguing question of why anyone wants to *know* how many postmen were bitten by dogs in a three-year period, and what he proposed to do with the answer when he'd got it – how did the PMG happen to have these statistics at his fingertips? I'm assuming he didn't just make them up, which is what I'd have done in his shoes.

Presumably all postmen who get bitten by dogs fill in some kind of a report and this, I imagine, goes to some central department. Now is there a clerk who spends his days filing and image seems far-fetched. I seem to hear the low-pitched hum of dog and type of injury sustained?

Even in the near-imbecile world of the Civil Service, the image seems far-fetched. I seem to hear the low-pitched hum of the computer – and furthermore a computer *that has nothing better to do with its time.*

Because the whole point about those wretched machines, as they themselves never tire of telling us, is that they are capable of one hundred thousand arithmetical calculations a second. A computer can produce more statistics than anyone knows what to do with in the time it takes the managing director to go up in the office lift, and it has the rest of the day to spare playing noughts and crosses, making up poems and all the other stupid things that computers are supposed to be able to do.

There is a woman from the Board of Trade who prowls about the departure lounge of London Airport accosting passengers. She wants to know where they are going, who is paying for their flights, how long they'll be away and the purpose of their journey.

I once asked this lady – having told her that I was going to the Fiji Islands for the funeral of a celebrated accordion player, and that my flight was being paid for by the Rotary Club of Pontefract – what in God's name the Board of Trade did with this information. She said they fed it into a computer. I asked her what happened to it then, and she didn't know. What was more impressive, she didn't care.

Nobody really wants to know why 115 people flew out of England on a Boeing 707 on August 5 last year. Nobody really cares how many postmen were bitten by dogs in 1967, except possibly the postmen themselves. But the computer is there. And it fully intends to go on producing facts that will get more bizarre as the years go by until someone gives it a good swift kick.

Does anyone know how many thousands of tons of useless information will be clogging up our desks and filing cabinets by the end of the century? The computers could tell us in one-fifth of a second. And then, since they're so clever, perhaps they could all take themselves off to the pictures.

The Way We Live Now

I don't know how planners and architects spend their evenings. Playing with matchboxes, most likely. They could do worse, tomorrow night at 10.30, than watch a programme on ITV.

It is a film by Ken Ashton called 'We Was All One' and it is about how life has changed for the people of Bermondsey.

They once lived huddled together in a jumble of mean streets between the markets and the docks. Everyone knew everyone and when the corner shop was closed, which was not often, you borrowed your cup of sugar from the folks next door.

All that was before they were correctly organised. Nowadays they live in high-rise blocks of flats, they have their proper ration of communal open space, no one knows anybody, and – for the older people at least – life is pretty bloody miserable.

What has happened to Bermondsey has also happened to neighbourhoods throughout Britain. The best that can be said about the few remaining communities where the old life still goes on is that although the clammy hand of redevelopment has not grabbed them yet, it will grab them soon.

The planners and architects have not learned, and show no signs of learning, that although their matchboxes may be pleasing to the eye, the people obliged to live in them are somewhat more complicated than matchstick-men.

True, it is beginning to dawn upon some of them that the craze for tower blocks was probably the biggest gaffe in the bricks-and-mortar game since the Leaning Tower of Pisa. On past evidence, all they will learn from this big mistake is how to make a bigger one.

There are a hundred reasons why blueprint communities, such as the new Bermondsey, work on paper but not in practice. Too much theorising, too much regard for passing fads, too much meddling, too much contempt for established values.

The main trouble is that the planners insist on planning what cannot be planned. They are like the Irish barber who offered his clients two shaves at one sitting because he wanted a day off.

I wish I could take a few of them on one of my favourite walks which takes me along a tumbledown street on the fringe of Bloomsbury. It would give them heartburn to look at it but they might learn something.

Architecturally speaking, it is a disaster area. The houses are too tall for the length of the street except for those that are too small for the width of it; together they form a skyline resembling an unfinished jigsaw. The green tiles of the pub – a monument to bad taste in its own right – do not go well with the blue plastic front of the betting shop next door.

By all the planners' rules, the street makes no sense at all. Clearly such a small community can support only one news-agent: this one has two. Obviously the fumes from the Indian restaurant must annoy the local residents: yet this Indian restaurant seems to be the local residents' favourite place. The greengrocer's stall is obstructing the public highway: no one seems to mind.

In any well-planned neighbourhood the tailor's workshop should be on a factory estate and not on the ground floor of a private house. The pub should stand on its own site with proper parking facilities. The launderette should be in a recognised service area. The houses should all look as if they were built in the same year. There should be less asphalt and more grass.

And indeed, if you leave the green-tiled pub by the saloon bar door and turn right then left and walk on a bit, you will arrive at just such a well-planned neighbourhood. It is an interesting complex of pedestrian walk-ways, footbridges and large concrete basins containing tulips. The difference between it and the potty little street I have described is that the street is alive and the nearby housing development, which has come to replace it, is dead. Or rather, stillborn.

Planners tend to dismiss our wistful affection for corner shops, ugly pubs and the old gas-lamp as cheap nostalgia. The fact remains that these streets worked; theirs don't.

Architects are perhaps slightly more in touch with common life, but only in theory. Although they are all for bustling arcades and jolly piazzas, the *joie de vivre* never seems to get off the drawing-board. Nor will it ever, until they see that places get their life from people; it can never happen the other way about.

Designing cities is a lost art. The Venetians have Venice, which is now sinking into the lagoon. New Yorkers have New York, which is falling to pieces. Londoners have London, Loiners have Leeds, Mancunians have Manchester, Liverpudlians have Liverpool, Brummies have Birmingham. They will not have these well-loved cities much longer if they don't watch out.

A Man From The North

Lolling at my café table (Yes, thanks, but it rained on the Tuesday), I have been reading, with very great pleasure, Margaret Drabble's new biography of Arnold Bennett.

It gave me pleasure not only because this Drabble writes like a dream, and I shouldn't be surprised if she took it up for a living, but because I have been a Bennett fan for as long as I can remember. (And so will you be, when the forthcoming TV serial of 'Clayhanger' fills the gap left by 'The Forsyte Saga'.)

Should you happen to come to my house, you will find in the left-hand shelves by the fireplace nearly every book that Arnold Bennett ever wrote – ninety-odd titles in all. Browsers are welcome, but if you try to make away with my treasured edition of 'The Old Wives' Tale' you will never reach the front door.

I will tell you what is so special about this volume. It is a facsimile of Bennett's original manuscript in his own handwriting, complete with crossings-out, and only five hundred copies of it exist. But it is more than a literary curiosity. It has an interesting story which – and it's no use looking at your watch in that marked manner – I am about to tell you.

You probably know that Arnold Bennett was an absolutely prodigious writer. It was a thin year for him if he didn't rattle off two or three novels, a couple of plays, half a dozen short stories and twenty or thirty newspaper articles.

He was also the complete professional. No temperament about our Arnold. 'The author,' he wrote, 'is in essence the same thing as a grocer . . . Fiction is sold and bought just like any other fancy goods . . .' (Those of you who ask me how to get into this writing game should read 'The Truth About An Author', which contains much sturdy advice on these lines. But copies are scarce, and you can't borrow mine.)

So when this Tommy Lipton of the Five Towns decided it was high time he added a masterpiece to his stock of literary provisions, he didn't mess about taking long walks on the seashore by moonlight, looking for inspiration. He simply dropped a line to his publisher to say that he was writing a 200,000-word serious novel and it would be ready by September 15.

Then he sat down and got on with it.

If you have read 'The Old Wives' Tale', and I hope you have, you must think it represents about five years' work. In fact, it took the industrious Arnold well under a year (he finished it on August 30, two weeks before his deadline). And in the same period he wrote two other novels, a play, two books of popular philosophy, six short stories – including 'A Matador in the Five Towns', which is a little gem – and sixty articles.

But we still haven't come to the point of the story. Understandably enough, some of Arnold Bennett's friends were worried that he was driving himself too hard, and one of them suggested that he should relax a little and take up a hobby. He thought this a sound idea and plumped for calligraphy – the art of fancy penmanship as once practised by monks. When I tell you that this new interest coincided with the start of 'The Old Wives' Tale', you will probably gues what is coming.

Yes. He wrote the whole of that mammoth work – 650 pages of manuscript – in a beautiful, mad, painstaking, obsessive copperplate, with coloured lettering at the head of each chapter, that would not be out of place under a glass case in a Carmelite monastery.

And that was our Arnold. When I see some of the present-day tribe of authors mewling about their problems on the television arts programmes, I think of him forming his scrolls and curlicues – with a calendar at his elbow.

Another sound reason for admiring Arnold Bennett, of course, is that he was a northerner – hence my headline. It was the title of his first novel.

I see that I have told you nothing at all about Margaret Drabble's biography. I think the best arrangement is for you to read it yourself. It was published by Weidenfeld & Nicolson at £4.95, which I agree is a lot of money even for a big, fat, splendid book. But you can get it from the library.

Miss Drabble says that she wrote it because she wanted to shake Arnold Bennett's hand; and I want to shake hers for giving me such enjoyment. If you, in turn, would like to shake my hand for putting you on to a good thing, there may be enough of us to form a human chain around the Five Towns.

Marching Orders

I'll tell you exactly what we are going to do during the Easter holidays. First of all we are going to stop cramming chocolate down our throats as if we were the All-England finalists in the Billy Bunter Guzzling Marathon.

Secondly we are going to pick up all those bits of silver paper. Every scrap. Now.

Thirdly, one of us is going to hose down the baby. I hope everyone realises that that child has just consumed its own weight in cream-filled Easter eggs?

Fourthly we are going to stop whining, grizzling, standing on one foot and complaining of stomach-ache, and we are going to listen.

The plan is this. We are going hiking.

That is the word I used. Hiking. Hands up all those who know what hiking is.

Very well then, as I appear to be surrounded by a collection of chocolate-coated ignoramuses who do not understand their own mother tongue, I will endeavour to explain.

If you will glance down at the carpet – which I might observe in passing still looks like Cadbury's packing department – you will see that each of you is in possession of certain protuberances covered in scuffed leather.

These are called feet.

Those of you who can count will notice that these feet are two in number. By putting foot A in front of foot B, you will find that your body is propelled forward. You may recall experimenting on these lines when the car was laid up last August.

The process I have just described is known as walking. When it is employed for long distances – as it might be a twenty-mile tramp across open country – it is known as hiking.

Hiking, as opposed to sitting in stuffy cinemas or riding about in motor cars, is what we are going to do this Easter.

I shall want you all ready, knapsacks packed, at 6 a.m. promptly, come rain or shine. Those of you who are unable to keep this appointment are always free to go and play marbles on the M1.

Stop that snivelling at once. Good God, when I was your age the Easter hike was as much a part of everyday life as that wretched telly is now. Incidentally, if the baby is hell-bent on electrocuting itself, it has only got to continue sucking that horizontal hold.

Now what we have here is an Ordnance Survey map. We shall leave the car at this point here and set off along that lane there. We will go across those fields, up that hill, through those woods, around that pond, over that ploughed field, through that bog, along that path, and be back where we started shortly before nightfall.

I will tell you exactly what is the point of setting off in the first place. It is to get some fresh air in our lungs and some colour in our cheeks. You look like so many lumps of uncooked pastry, the lot of you.

There will be no question of any of you sitting in the car reading comics until the rest of us get back. Comics are barred on this expedition. So, if it comes to that, are chocolate eggs whether milk or plain. We will take wholesome refreshment in the way of bread and cheese.

The baby will have bread and cheese and like it. Any child that can knock back a pound and a half of nougat before breakfast can eat anything. That baby is a human ostrich.

I am glad that someone has raised that point. I fully agree that, owing to a mixture of indolence and low cunning, the baby is unable to walk. It will have to be carried.

We will take it in turns. One of you will carry the baby across the fields and up the hill, another will convey it through the woods and I will carry it around the pond. I may as well warn the baby here and now that if it insists on dribbling during our Easter hike as it is dribbling at present, it will finish up head-first *in* the pond.

Are there any questions?

'I feel sick' is not a question, it is a statement of fact. In any case, it is completely irrelevant to the invigorating adventure on which we are about to embark.

You cannot take Mr Golliwog, no.

It is a matter of supreme indifference to me whether Mr Golliwog will cry if he is left behind or not. For all I care he can hang himself with piano wire. This is a serious outing.

Oh, very well then, Mr Golliwog can come on condition that he wears his dubbined boots like the rest of us. Any more questions?

We will not get lost. We will not be tossed by a mad bull. We will not be sucked into the bog. We will not be kidnapped by the gypsies in the wood.

And one thing further. The first child to whine about feeling tired will also have cause to whine about feeling the back of my hand. I have planned this hike for your enjoyment, and enjoy it you will, so help me God.

Such Is Fame

I do most of my work in a semi-basement room that is over-looked from the street. Sitting at my desk this morning, I became aware of a gaggle of schoolboys peering down at me through the railings as if I were a newly-arrived panda at the zoo.

And I heard this piping conversation:

'There's that bloke. Him what's always typing.'

'What's he type, then?'

'He's a writer, stupid! He types out his writing.'

'What's he write, then?'

'Dunno. I fink he writes jokes.'

I suppose there are worse epitaphs.